Daley.
Observations

Daley Observations

The Best of C.R. Daley's WESTERN RECORDER Editorials

Edited by A.B. Colvin and Mark Wingfield

PROVIDENCE HOUSE PUBLISHERS
Franklin, Tennessee

Copyright 1998 by *Western Recorder, Inc.*

Printed in the United States of America

02   01   00   99   98   1   2   3   4   5

Library of Congress Catalog Card Number: 98-67674

ISBN: 1-57736-122-9

Cover design by Gary Bozeman

Published by
PROVIDENCE HOUSE PUBLISHERS
238 Seaboard Lane • Franklin, Tennessee 37067
800-321-5692

Dedicated to
Christine Daley
and the Daley children,
Gil, Mike, Dale, and Phil

CONTENTS

FOREWORD

FROM 1957 THROUGH 1984, THOUSANDS OF Kentuckians faithfully followed the writing of Chauncey R. Daley. As editor of the *Western Recorder*, America's second-oldest Baptist newspaper, Daley became both a prophetic voice and a compassionate voice in homes and churches across the Commonwealth.

This collection of his best editorials demonstrates why at the time of his retirement he was hailed as the "dean" of state Baptist newspaper editors. His courage and conviction, combined with an easy-to-read writing style, gained attention well beyond the borders of Kentucky.

Now, more than 40 years after he began writing editorials, his words still carry penetrating insights. In reading this book, should you fail to look closely at the publication date on some editorials, you might mistakenly think they were written yesterday. On others, you will be reminded of how things have changed in our culture in the last half-century. Though some of the language used in the 1950s and '60s may sound peculiar today, Daley's words were written with compassion and kindness.

Daley wrote frequently and forcefully on the race issue, at a time when it was not fashionable for a white Baptist to be doing so. He and his family received harassment and threatening phone calls as a result. Yet he stuck by his convictions and in time was proved to be a prophet.

This book contains a sampling of those editorials, as well as a representative sampling of the many other topics he addressed through 27 years of editorial writing. Many other excellent editorials could have been included in this volume, but space would not permit a full accounting.

A word of thanks is due several people who made this book a reality. A.B. Colvin did the major research, rereading every editorial Daley wrote to cull out the cream of the crop. This was a monumental task, given that Daley sometimes wrote two or three editorials for each of the 1,350 issues he edited over 27 years. The selected editorials then were rekeyed by Shirley Wooton and Ann Tatum, who worked diligently to ensure that history was preserved accurately. Thanks also to Charles Deweese of Providence House Publishers for expediting publication on a short schedule.

Of course, the current *Western Recorder* staff and board of directors extend heartfelt thanks to the entire Daley family for allowing us to create this book and to establish the C.R. and Christine Daley Endowment Fund, which will benefit from proceeds from the sale of the book.

Finally, my personal gratitude goes to Chauncey Daley himself. As one of his successors in the editor's seat at the *Western Recorder*, I am amazed and humbled to follow in such gigantic footsteps. The legacy of the Daley years with the *Western Recorder* is rich, and it is a resource from which we all continue to benefit.

His example inspires us to honor the words of Scripture that to this day adorn the masthead of every issue: "Earnestly contend for the faith which was once for all delivered to the saints."

Mark Wingfield
June 1998

INTRODUCTION

MORE THAN A DECADE OF REWARDING MINISTRY
as a teacher of Greek and Latin at Georgetown College and
two years of fruitful leadership as pastor of Harrodsburg Baptist
Church preceded C.R. Daley's becoming editor of the *Western
Recorder* in 1957.

Confessing no journalistic background and no plans, long-
range or short-range, he was fully aware of the critical time of
history which was all around him. He recognized the unique faith
and convictions resident among Kentucky Baptists.

Declaring truth in reporting and sincerity in interpretation of
events his guiding principles, he promised that whatever he wrote
would be honest, sincere, and personal convictions. He prayed
for wisdom like that of Solomon as he began the work which was
to continue for 27 years.

May these selected samples stir the same challenges and
inspirations in today's reader they did in readers from 1957 to
1984.

In his closing editorial, Daley expressed his gratitude to
Kentucky Baptist congregations, organizations, agencies and
institutions, fellow Kentucky Baptist Building colleagues, *Western*

Recorder directors and fellow workers in the office, and to his most faithful supporter and most valuable critic, his wife, Christine.

To express to God his happy remembrances and hearty gratitude, he wrote, "The lines have fallen unto me in pleasant places," quoting Psalm 16:6. May you, the reader, be aware of this spirit and your inclusion in it and your kinship to it as you read these pages.

A.B. Colvin

REFLECTIONS OF A NEW EDITOR
(C.R. DALEY'S FIRST EDITORIAL)

SOME HAVE CALLED IT AN HONOR; OTHERS SAY it's a promotion; a few regard it as the opposite; some even refer to it as a retirement, but by far the most who have expressed themselves see in it a great opportunity for Kingdom service. I haven't recovered sufficiently from the shock to know exactly how to consider the election as editor of the *Western Recorder*, but this one thing I'm convinced of: Whatever else it is, it is the inscrutable, inexplicable will of God which moves his creatures with or without the sanction of human reason. Without journalistic background or many of the other prerequisites as the world regards qualifications, and without a wildest dream of even being editor of a state Baptist paper, here I am. I confess I have no long-range plans—not even any short-range plans. I do have some ideas by now, some of which seem judicious and others which certainly would qualify as brainstorms. I know that at this point there are few things one could say as a new editor that he would not want to or have to take back later; nevertheless, there are some convictions which I am reasonably certain I'll cling to from now to the end, be it soon or late.

The first is that my work shall be a ministry as much as was the classroom of Georgetown College or the pulpit of Harrodsburg Baptist Church. The same sense of divine guidance that took me to Georgetown and Harrodsburg has brought me here. When I left college teaching I felt nothing could ever give the same sense of fulfillment, and now I am just as certain that no place could ever give the same soul satisfaction as the personal pastoral ministry. I'm leaving what gives me all I could ever desire in happiness and a church which is a preacher's dream. Nothing less than a consciousness of God's command would budge me.

The next conviction is that with the responsibility of editorship of the *Western Recorder* comes a heritage without parallel. The paper has occupied a place in religious journalism which is truly unique. Of its editors I have known only the present retiring servant of God. In my judgment Dr. Skinner's work has been forthright, fair, progressive and exemplary in every way, and I know it will be a matter of little feet to fit big shoes, but his own kind and encouraging word will be of inestimable value to me.

Another conviction of my soul is that no hour of history has been more critical for God's people called Baptists than this one. It ranks in my mind with the hour when Jesus commissioned the church with task or when Carey was ignited by God to set Baptists on missionary fire or when Judson and Rice saw right by New Testament light. The spiritual destiny of this world might well be determined by the response of Baptists to God in this generation. The place of this publication in that destiny is my soul's concern.

A belief of great comfort to me is that Baptist faith and convictions are found nowhere in finer or truer form than among Kentucky Baptists. With all the nobility of Baptists everywhere there is something about Kentucky Baptists that is distinct, different and grand, and my 13 years among them have made me a great debtor. Dr. George Rangland used to say it exactly as I feel it: "For Baptist orthodoxy to die Kentucky Baptists would have to die first." I say this with full realization that Baptists in every place have privilege to the same feeling.

As to my own expressions on this page or elsewhere in the *Recorder*, I can only promise that whatever is said will be honest, sincere and personal convictions. Truth in reporting and sincerity in interpretation of events will be my guiding principle whatever the costs. If I praise, it will be honest; if I criticize or question, it will be with good intentions. I will always be willing to speak the truth as I am given power to know it and trust my fate to God and to Kentucky Baptists. I beseech your prayers, brethren, and your mercy. My prayer today and every day ahead is and will be that of Solomon in his dream, "I am but a little child. I know not how to go out or come in. . . . Give therefore thy servant an understanding heart . . . for who is able to judge this thy so great a people?" (July 11, 1957)

DALEY OBSERVATIONS ON RACE

"I WAS AN HUNGERED, AND...,"
OR, TWO CANDY BARS AND TO BED

IT ALL BEGAN AT THE KENTUCKY BAPTIST STUDENT Union Convention in Lexington. On the Saturday evening program were two truly great humanitarians. One was Dr. Robert Hingston, professor of anesthesia at Western Reserve University. The other was Henry Q. Taylor, secretary of Health Services for the nation of Liberia, in West Africa. The two famous men came to tell 1,000 or more Kentucky Baptist college youth about Operation Brothers Brother II. This project which was inspired by Dr. Hingston saw the dread disease of smallpox begun to be brought under control by mass inoculation of thousands in the cities and bush of Liberia. This was possible because a team of doctors and technicians gave their time and services in this mission of mercy. The inoculations were done with the famous peace gun, invented by Dr. Hingston. It shoots serum at 700 miles per hour painlessly into the arms of patients as fast as they pass by.

Dr. Hingston is a member of the First Baptist Church of Cleveland. He was born and reared in Alabama and is a medical genius. He believes he is to use his medical skill and personal resources for ridding the underprivileged peoples of the world of the diseases for which there is a cure. He asked for and received a million dollars worth of serum from American drug companies and from other sources received hundreds of tons of Bibles and books for distribution among Liberians.

In Liberia, Hingston was welcomed and aided in the project by Health Secretary Taylor. They worked tirelessly 14 to 18 hours a day inoculating, removing goiters and performing other acts of healing mercy. At Hingston's insistence, Taylor has come to the United States for a visit, with Hingston as his host. Since arriving, Taylor has spent time at medical schools, other health centers and in Washington where he has had conferences with such high U.S. officials as G. Mennen Williams, secretary for Africa in the Kennedy administration.

At Hingston's suggestion, Taylor told the students how he had already succeeded in ridding Liberia of the dread disease called yaws. This disease is caused by a syphilitic-type germ which eats large pockets in the victim's body. One shot of penicillin kills the germ. Taylor, a radiant Christian, belongs to the Lutheran Church and is currently running for the national congress in Liberia. Imagine the privilege of bringing these two famous humanitarians back to Louisville by auto from Lexington. But the thrill of being in the company of these two great men soon turned into humiliation.

Starting out from Lexington about 11 p.m., Taylor mentioned that he was hungry, since he had not eaten anything since breakfast. He had missed lunch on his plane, which could not even land in Lexington due to the fog. Deplaning in Louisville, he rushed to the convention in Lexington, arriving after his scheduled time on the program.

The first eating place open as we journeyed toward Louisville was in Frankfort. As we walked into this place, it never occurred to me that one of us had different color skin. In fact, from the moment that I met this great person I was never aware of his color. But I was suddenly jarred to reality when I saw the anguished face of the waitress when we sat down.

Immediately I went to her to explain who we were and why we needed to eat. She had already sent for the man in charge who appeared and expressed regrets that he could not serve us. He said this was a community policy, and he was instructed by the restaurant owner not to serve a colored person. We departed, assuring our friend Louisville was different in this respect.

We arrived at the Louisville hotel at 1:15 a.m., just after the coffee shop had closed. Taylor was still hungry from not eating in 18 hours, and so we found an all-night eating place two blocks away. Feeling certain it was all right, but wishing to avoid any scene, I went in ahead to ask about service. Again, the man in charge shook his head saying the boss had left orders not to feed any black customers.

And so Hingston and Taylor said goodbye and walked back to the hotel and to bed still without even a hamburger. Two bars of candy bought by a white man was all the food a famous humanitarian had on his first visit to Kentucky.

I felt like crying, not for Taylor who smiled through it all, but for Kentuckians who apparently never read, "Be not forgetful to entertain strangers: for thereby some have entertained angels unawares" (Hebrews 13:2).

You see, Liberia had meant much more than they realized to these who had not even a crumb for a distinguished Liberian. Liberia fought with the United States in World Wars I and II. In World War II American troops were stationed in Liberia to keep Germany and her allies from using the coastal region as a base of operation. It was also from Liberia that almost every pound of rubber came that kept America's military machines on wheels. And Taylor's fellow countrymen had served as American beasts of burden in transporting this rubber on their heads to the loading places. If Germany instead of America had gotten

Liberian rubber, Germans might be treating Americans today like Kentuckians treated a Liberian last Saturday night. Probably those refusing to feed Taylor rode home last Saturday night from work on rubber from Liberia.

Besides all this, there is a consideration of such pointed words as: "Depart from me, ye cursed, into everlasting fire, prepared for the devil and his angels: For I was an hungered and ye gave me no meat..."

"Lord, when saw we thee hungered ... and did not minister unto thee?"

"Verily, I say unto you, inasmuch as ye did it not to one of the least of these, ye did it not to me."

And these shall go away into everlasting punishment. (November 29, 1962)

WILL SOUTHERN BAPTISTS FIDDLE
WHILE AMERICA BURNS?

UP UNTIL RECENTLY, PREDICTIONS HAVE pictured the 1968 Southern Baptist Convention as another routine convention with the selection of a successor to President Franklin Paschall as about the most interesting item. These predictions had better not be true. If Southern Baptist do business as usual this year in Houston, we may well be out of business in a short time so far as being an influential force in American life. The movements in modern American life and the dramatic events in recent days make 1968 one of the truly crucial periods in Southern Baptist history.

There is much that is right about Southern Baptists, and we can be justifiably proud of much of our record. But in one area we have miserably failed up to now, and our whole future may rest on what we do about this failure. This is the area of our attitude and our action toward our Negro brothers and their human rights.

In the struggle of American Negroes for equal opportunity and first-class citizenship Southern Baptists have done almost nothing. We have refused not only to work for full rights for black Americans ourselves, but in many instances we have actually resisted the efforts of others in the struggle for full emancipation.

Now the times demand that Southern Baptists be counted for or against a new day of freedom and justice for American Negroes. The world must know where we stand on the burning issues that hourly threaten to plunge America into a holocaust of destruction and a bloodbath of interracial war.

We must no longer justify our silence with high-sounding arguments. One of these is historic Baptist polity which puts so much emphasis on local autonomy and independence that no Baptist speaks for another nor any Baptist group for the rest of Baptists. This is a precious part of our heritage and must be preserved, but we can no longer hide behind it in our silence. At least Baptists who gather at Houston can speak for themselves. And since the vast majority of all Baptists at the convention will be pastors and their wives, their voices will be significant.

Another reason given for non-involvement by many Southern Baptists in the human rights struggle is their objections to many policies and methods employed by civil rights leaders. To many of us, many methods employed have been highly objectionable and even unchristian and could not be endorsed. But we must not forsake the ideals while rejecting the methods. Let us join the struggle, choosing our own methods in keeping with our own convictions.

Southern Baptists in Houston should take two monumental steps. One is to come forth with a loud and clear voice sounding our convictions on human rights. This voice should be so sharp and strong that no one hearing it could ever doubt where we stand.

The other step that should be taken will be much more difficult. This is to implement these convictions with an educational

program directed to all Southern Baptists to overcome our traditional prejudices and come to the practice of love and fellowship
which know no color distinctions. For this step there must be
divine transformation as well as human education. It's a pious
sounding suggestion, but the only hope for many of us in this
matter is the miracle of God's power to change our thinking. Let
every Baptist who prays stay in the closet with God until he has
God's mind on this matter.

Such heart searching will necessarily produce heartbreaks.
Some good people will never change their basic attitudes in this
life toward the Negro. This means that to take a stand will in
some instances put brother against brother, congregation against
pastor, father against son and even husband against wife.

More pastors will have to go as some have already gone. To be
headless and right, however, is better than to be secure and wrong.
Denominational leaders must be fearless for God's sake rather
than fearful for position's sake. They must be climate-makers and
not climate-reflectors. This will be at the cost of being branded
modernists, liberals and even Communists. Furthermore, some
loss of denominational revenue due to withholding of contributions can also be expected. Our denominational unity will be
seriously strained if not broken. This is a high price but it must be
paid, if necessary. Too long we have protected denominational
harmony by compromise and silence.

America is on fire. Will Southern Baptists fiddle while it
burns? God has been more long-suffering with us than we have
deserved. This is our great moment of truth. If we fail we need
not ask for whom the bells toll. We can be sure they toll for us.
(May 9, 1968)

FOR WHOM THE JUDGMENT BELLS TOLL

SUNDAY, SEPTEMBER 15, 1963, WILL FOREVER BE one of the darkest days in American history. It's almost impossible to believe the truth. Four innocent American children were ruthlessly murdered by fellow Americans, and this while the children were studying the Holy Bible in their own church. For this to happen in a land more than 300 years after it was founded for the sake of freedom and equality almost defies the imagination.

It's easy to assess blame and accuse someone else for such a tragic sin. It is harder to realize corporate responsibility and repent as a nation of people.

Those in Birmingham find some comfort in blaming it all on the Supreme Court, the national administration and agitation from outsiders. Outsiders, unfamiliar with the total situation, can point a pharisaical finger toward Birmingham while overlooking similar or other sins in their own backyard. The fact is all of us have sown the seeds which have brought such a sad harvest.

To say such a deed is representative of all of the people of Birmingham would be grossly false. But to say attitudes and actions of responsible citizens who themselves would never stoop so low did not encourage the lunatic fringe to such depths would also be false.

There have been voices unheeded that might well have been heeded. *Alabama Baptist* editor Leon Macon, whose words reach 100,000 or more Alabama Baptist families every week, spoke clearly and loudly on the side of law and order in the crisis. Some Baptist pastors and other preachers spoke as bravely and at the greatest personal hazard. But the reality of the tragedy still haunts us.

This black Sunday is a judgment upon Birmingham. It is judgment upon a society built on the philosophy of white supremacy. It is judgment upon outsiders who blamed insiders, and insiders who blamed outsiders. It is judgment upon America founded for freedom and equality of every race and color. It is judgment upon unscrupulous politicians willing to grow fat and powerful upon the blood of the innocent.

But more than upon anyone else, Sunday, September 15, 1963, is judgment upon people called Baptists. There are more Baptists in Birmingham and elsewhere in the South than any other people claiming relationship with Jesus Christ. More people through the years have listened to more Baptist preaching than to any other voices speaking for God. Baptists must bear the greatest responsibility because they have enjoyed the greatest opportunity.

Great and mighty Baptist churches dot the Birmingham skyline, and even as bodies were mangled and blood spilt in the basement of one Baptist church, thousands of Baptists were in Bible study and worship services in other Baptist churches in Birmingham and across the nation. What did the Bible they studied and the sermons they heard say about injustice, intolerance and murder?

And while the smell of dynamite lingers and the soil is fresh upon the graves of innocent children, hundreds of Baptist district associations across the land are in session as is the Southern Baptist Convention Executive Committee in Nashville. What will be talked about in these Baptist gatherings? In the corridors and churchyards remarks about the tragedy of Birmingham will be exchanged, but this will be soon forgotten as we use Baptist statistics to prove we are God's chosen as we make careful plans to keep the offerings higher than last year.

But still the blood of Birmingham cries out. At whose hands will it be required? How long will Southern Baptists be satisfied only to go on raising a million and more dollars a day to help keep up our far-flung enterprise while justice, mercy and love go begging? When will we lay down our robes of respectability and popular approval and our money bags of success for the sackcloth and ashes of repentance? What will it profit a denomination if it gains the whole world and loses its own soul? September 15, 1963, is not only a sad day in the history of the United States of America. It's a sad day in Southern Baptist history. (September 26, 1963)

BAPTIST IDEALS AND MARTIN LUTHER KING

THE RECENT ASSASSINATION OF MARTIN LUTHER King Jr., had an unprecedented impact upon America. It dominated the news for five full days and even pushed the Vietnam peace efforts to a secondary place. Few would have predicted such a tremendous reaction to the death of one American, especially a Negro.

Many religious groups and leaders spoke out and identified themselves with the ideals of the martyred Negro leader. Hundreds of memorial services were held all over the land, but one religious group was noticeable for its almost complete absence from participation in the public mourning for Dr. King.

Except for widely-scattered instances, Southern Baptists were silent on this historic occasion. Baptist spokesmen expressed regret for the tragedy when asked by reporters, and at least two Baptist pastors joined in the Memphis march and rally on the day before the King funeral. But on the whole, Southern Baptists treated Dr. King's death as untouchable as they did his life and ministry.

The day-long televised funeral service in Atlanta showed a veritable array of political and religious leadership of the United States. Everybody but white Baptists seemed to be there. Governors from far away came, but the Baptist governor from Georgia stayed away and had himself protected with armed guards.

There is a strange irony about the absence of white Baptists in memorial services and in the tribute paid to Martin Luther

King. After all, he was a Baptist. Why should other religious groups recognize his ideals and courage while Baptists ignore them? Not only was he a Baptist, but the great majority of all black people in America are Baptists. It is estimated that 60 percent of all Negro church members are members of Baptist churches. This percentage will likely not be this high very long.

A sadder truth is that the ideals King lived and died for are Baptist ideals. No doubt his life and mission were greatly influenced by the insights of his early life as a Baptist. For Baptists have been known through history as champions of freedom and defenders of justice. In much of our history we were the disfranchised, the persecuted and the poor. Our interpretation of the Scriptures has led us to stress the sacredness of human personality and the dignity of every individual.

Could it be that Baptists provided the insights and dreams for Martin Luther King, only to reject him when he sought to bring them to realization? Why have we preached equality and justice for all, only to deny it to the black people?

Part of the explanation is that we have been influenced more by culture than by the Bible. Southern Baptists began as a denomination and flourished in a culture that condoned slavery of blacks, and after slavery was officially abolished we still treated Negroes as inferiors and relegated them to be hewers of wood and drawers of water. We even found scriptural justification for their racial, social and economic inferiority.

It's high time as Baptists we recovered our historic witness to the worth of every man and the equality of opportunity for all persons of all colors. How ironic that most Negroes are Baptists and fellow Baptists are about the last to champion their full rights. Let's repent and be in the front instead of the rear in this righteous crusade. (April 25, 1968)

MAKING THE NEW ORDER A REALITY

SUNDAY, FEBRUARY 13, IS RACE RELATIONS Sunday for Southern Baptists. It behooves us to come to grips with what our religion has to do with race relations. In our own state we have reason for optimism. Thursday, January 27, was a truly historic day in Kentucky. The signing of the Kentucky Civil Rights Bill by Gov. Edward Breathitt made Kentucky the first Southern state to pass strong civil rights legislation. Coupled with the national civil rights legislation, the Kentucky legislation leaves little to be desired in the way of laws.

In a few brief years the race revolution has made remarkable strides in America. We are too close to it to realize it fully, but doubtless the 20th century revolution of oppressed peoples of the world will be judged even more significant than the American Revolution or the French Revolution.

The old order had to go in America as it has in other parts of the world. The dream of equality had grown in the womb of the black race for many years. Like a child when the time of birth comes, this freedom dream could not be held back. The birth pains have been severe but birth must come even if the mother dies in labor.

And so the new order has appeared. The biggest task, however, is still ahead. This is to make the new order a reality in spirit and truth. Legislation can never do this, through it is a necessary part of the process.

The true realization of the dream of justice and equality is a matter of men's hearts, and hearts are never changed by law. Only God can change hearts and only the love which results can make perfect the new order. Rights may be aided by law, but right prevails ultimately only by love.

This gives reason for hope, especially in the South. The number of whites and blacks in the South who have sincere trust in God is legion, and there is no reason not to believe they will learn to live in the new order on the level of Christian love. Whites and blacks in the South worship and love the same God. They have in the main loved one another though they differed on God's plan for the Negro in this world.

The new order must say goodbye to the kind of peace based on a paternalistic attitude of whites toward blacks. This is gone forever though many whites look back on it as the golden age and many blacks were satisfied with it and still are. An attitude of condescension is not real love. Real love is based not on the worth of another, say nothing of his color, but upon the fact that he was made in God's image and is redeemed by the blood of Jesus just as I am. When this love comes, both white and blacks can truly sing "We Have Overcome." (February 10,1966)

WILL KENTUCKY BAPTISTS SET INTEGRATION EXAMPLE?

NOW THAT THERE ARE SOME INTEGRATED Baptist churches in Kentucky, what can we expect in the way of a trend and what influence will Kentucky have upon other sections of the Southern Baptist Convention territory?

Kentucky is a key state and might well be a laboratory for the rest of the convention. There are other states in the West or north of the Mason-Dixon with Southern Baptist work where integration is more advanced, but of the traditionally Southern states, Kentucky is further along in the matter of integration than any other. Virginia Baptists, for example, are considered quite progressive in many respects but Virginia is one of the most reactionary states on the integration issue.

School integration has been effected in Kentucky with little difficulty, and Louisville has been cited as a model city in school integration. This would seem to indicate church integration could follow smoothly.

Actually, outside of scattered examples, very little has taken place to indicate any likelihood of integration on any large scale among Kentucky Baptist churches. So far there has been little occasion for integration of churches.

Negro Baptists number about 150,000 in Kentucky. They have a fine organization with good leadership. Mutual respect and fine relations exist between the leadership of General Association of Colored Baptists and the leadership of the 600,000 white Baptists in Kentucky.

This seems little reason to expect any agitation for church integration in Kentucky on a large scale. Most communities have Negro churches greatly loved and cherished by their own members who would be as reluctant to leave their home church as most Baptists are. Each white and Negro church has a program of worship fitted to the social, educational and cultural level of the congregation and wholesale change would not be satisfactory or satisfying.

Some sections of Kentucky, like the east, north and central, have small populations of Negroes with somewhat high social and educational levels. In these communities church integration just as school integration will be more needed and generally accepted. In other sections of Kentucky, like southern and western, are more Negroes and a more Deep-South culture prevails. Here church integration seems unlikely anytime soon.

What can we expect then in Kentucky? In communities where Negro population is small, where Negro worship facilities are absent or inadequate, or where Negroes have advanced in social and educational status, church integration will definitely increase. In communities with considerable Negro population still below the community average level of social and educational status, the Negroes will remain in their own churches for a long time.

Some will object to these observations on the ground that too much is made of social and educational status because spiritual status supersedes these. This is altogether true, but the fact remains that most Baptist churches are conducted on the basis of and appeal to certain levels of social and educational status.

The chief difference between Kentucky and some of the other states of the Southern Baptist Convention in church integration seems to be that integration will take place smoothly but slowly in places where it is needed in Kentucky, but this is too much to expect anytime soon in the Deep South. (July 23, 1959)

A MEANINGFUL CONFERENCE

THE RECENT CONFERENCE BETWEEN REPRE-sentatives from the leading Negro and white Baptist conventions in Kentucky was characterized by a genuine spirit of understanding and cooperation. Such a meeting has been long overdue though relationships between Negro and white Baptists in our state have always been cordial.

It was proper that the Kentucky Baptist Convention take the initiative in inviting Negro brethren to join us in a search for more ways for meaningful cooperation. As the larger group with more resources and advantages, we should be the first to put what we have together with the valuable resources of these fellow Baptists to bring about something more valuable for both groups.

This does not mean a merger of the two groups into one convention is planned soon or anytime for that matter. This was not the purpose of the meeting. It remains to be seen sometime out in the future if joining the conventions together would be an advantage. In the meantime we can do many things together while retaining the many advantages of maintaining separate organizations. The point is, as one of the Negro brethren observed, that the day should come when we no longer think of "white Baptists" and "Negro Baptists" but of "Baptists." The spirit of this recent conference gives indication that this day might not be as far away as once thought. (January 27, 1966)

A CENTURY OF SERVICE FOR SIMMONS

ONE OF THE TRULY SIGNIFICANT OCCASIONS IN the history of Baptists in Kentucky took place June 4. It was the celebration of the 100th Anniversary of Simmons Bible College in Louisville, and Christine and I were the guests of Mr. and Mrs. William Rogers for the centennial banquet. Rogers, secretary of the Kentucky Baptist interracial department, was awarded an honorary doctor's degree at the Simmons commencement on the same day.

Alumni and friends of Simmons filled the main banquet room of Stouffer's Inn and also an overflow hall where hundreds participated by means of closed-circuit television. Some were turned away after the 750 capacity facilities were filled.

Homer Nutter, who is well-known to white Kentucky Baptists because of speaking appearances at the Kentucky Baptist Convention, served as toastmaster. He was in his usual rare form and demonstrated not only a monumental knowledge of Simmons but an imperishable love and devotion to this school where he began his ministerial training. He is one of many alumni who lend stature to the institution.

Only those who lived in former days in Kentucky where opportunities for blacks to go to college were almost nil can truly appreciate the contributions of Simmons. Until the repeal of the Day Law in recent years it was unlawful for blacks and whites to attend school together and for many years Simmons was the only school in Kentucky where blacks could earn recognized college degrees. Hundreds of black teachers qualified for certification with their training at Simmons.

In the century of service Simmons has produced its share of notable graduates. They are now scattered over the world and have filled influential places in arts, in education, in professions and in business as well as in the black ministry. With other schools with state support now filling the place once served by

this school, the Simmons curriculum is geared to training ministers and other church-related vocational workers.

To have been present for the occasion would have been an
enlightening and liberating experience for anyone with a conde-
scending attitude toward black Baptists in Kentucky. The
elegance and good taste in dress, the courteous and polite
conduct and the wisely planned and well executed program were
all models for such an occasion. Tears of joy and admiration could
not be kept back when I heard of men and women with the sound
of slave chains still ringing in their hearts being so determined to
seek emancipation from ignorance and to find their place in the
sun.

There is an indescribable feeling which comes from sharing
such an experience. Here's a people whose relationship with God
gives them an imperishable determination to be free and whose
American heritage endows them with the American dream.
Moreover, because these have not been fully realized they have
something for which to live and struggle. Such a motivation
seems to be absent in much of white America and in many white
Baptists today. The emancipation of blacks lies not in joining us
but our liberation lies in joining them in this struggle and dream
which is as sure to come to pass as there is a God. (June 16,
1973)

DALEY OBSERVATIONS ON SOUTHERN BAPTISTS

WESTERN RECORDER

THERE IS A GREATNESS ABOUT SOUTHERN BAPTISTS

RESORTING TO THE EXTREME IS ALMOST A universal fault. Whichever side we take on a matter, we tend to overstate the case. This is surely true when it comes to how we think of ourselves as Baptists.

Up until several years ago Southern Baptists were about the biggest braggarts who could be found. We were leading all other religious groups in America in the rate of growth, in the number of young people responding to the call for full-time Christian service and in most other areas that can be statistically measured. To be sure, we said we gave God the credit but our chests were stuck out as we denied the credit. We were extreme in our self-appreciation.

Now it's just the opposite extreme. We have had a statistical decline and we have reacted like Chicken Little. The sky is falling and we outdo each other in castigating ourselves. Once we thought there was nothing wrong with Southern Baptists; now there is hardly anything we can find which is right about ourselves. Instead of saying Baptists are the hope of the world, we now are saying that God is the only hope for Baptists.

God is our only hope, and true humility is always becoming, but this should not lead us to complete self-depreciation. Somewhere between extreme self-appreciation and extreme self-depreciation lies the truth. Maybe we needed a statistical decline to deflate our Baptist ego. At the same time we don't need such self-castigation as is prevalent today.

With all our faults Baptists are a great people. Our greatness is not in statistical success but in the inner qualities we possess. Three of these qualities readily come to mind.

Baptists are great in their convictions. Contrary to what some observers say, Baptists are far from giving up their distinctives which are based upon divine revelation. This comes out wherever Baptist preaching is heard whether it be from the older or the younger generation of preachers. The younger generation of Baptist preachers tend not to use the old shibboleths and cliches nor emphasize provincial doctrinal positions, but neither do they buy the "God is dead" theology and the "new morality" ethics.

Baptists are great in their diversity. One of the amazing things about us is the variety of beliefs and practices. The formal worship services and the academic sermon in some Baptist churches is a million miles away from the simple, unstructured order of worship and the sermon from an untrained preacher of other Baptist churches.

To sit in a seminary classroom one day and to be present in a district association meeting in some section of Kentucky the next day is like being in two worlds. Yet the Baptist seminary professor and the non-trained Baptist preacher have enough conviction in common to belong together and enough respect for each other's differences to stay together. This is a part of the greatness of Southern Baptists.

Baptists are also great in their unity. This unity in diversity is possible only through love for and toleration of each other. It is one thing to be diverse, it's another thing to put up with each other when we don't agree. The temptation always is to pitch each other out, and the fact that Southern Baptists have remained together is a miracle. This miracle becomes even more amazing when we remember our unity is not in an ecclesiastical organization but only on the basis of voluntary cooperation. Only the help of the Lord and some degree of maturity in Southern Baptists can explain our unity within diversity.

Conviction, diversity and unity are but three of the inner qualities that make Southern Baptists what they are. Let us preserve these while purging ourselves of some traits which are not so commendable. (August 29, 1968)

THE BROADMAN BIBLE COMMENTARY

THE BROADMAN BIBLE COMMENTARY NOW IN process of preparation by Broadman Press stands to be one of the most significant contributions ever made to Baptists and to others by the Sunday School Board. Such an undertaking is long overdue and marks the coming of age of Southern Baptists in the field of biblical scholarship.

The first two volumes of the 12-volume work are scheduled for release October 1, 1969. These are Volume I, containing Genesis, Exodus and general articles on the Bible and the Old Testament, and Volume VIII containing Matthew-Mark and general articles on the New Testament. Each volume is priced at $7.50, and a reduced price of $77.50 is offered for the 12-volume set. The entire 12 volumes are scheduled for completion by the end of 1972.

Some of the best contemporary Baptist scholarship in America and England has been engaged to do this work. The general editor is Clifton Allen, one of the most perceptive minds and committed spirits among Southern Baptists. He will be assisted by an editorial board composed of a cross-section of Southern Baptist theological, denominational and pastoral leadership.

The work has been described as "integrity of interpretation by contemporary scholarship" and "trustworthy guidance toward understanding the biblical revelation." It will be all of this if present plans are fully realized.

General Editor Allen and the advisory board mean to let the writers be unfettered in their work. Responsible editing will be done, but no preconceived interpretation will be forced upon the writers. They are men of ability and integrity and will approach their task with whatever scientific tools of interpretation they have and with a commitment to and love for the Scriptures. This is the only way a respectable commentary can be produced.

The result is likely not to please every Baptist and will certainly upset those who make no room for any interpretation but their own. The choice of the Revised Standard Version for the text will be questioned by a few, but such recognition and use of this version by Southern Baptists is long overdue.

This set of commentaries is not to be considered the authorized Southern Baptist interpretation. There is so such thing now and hopefully there will never be. The commentaries will contain interpretations of honest, able and committed Baptists who are making a life study of the Scriptures. With some interpretations we will agree. With some we will disagree, and this is as it should be. After all, this is one of the ways we learn more of what God is saying to us today in the Bible, and this is the objective of the project. (August 1, 1968)

BAPTIST CONVENTIONS:
DEMOCRATIC OR DEMAGOGIC?

THE OLD AND CHERISHED BAPTIST PRACTICE OF providing for every church in the Southern Baptist Convention to be represented in the annual conventions might have to be looked at seriously. The democracy which this policy seeks to insure has been threatened by demagoguery in conventions of recent years.

The present method isn't accomplishing its purpose. Theoretically it provides for every local church to participate in convention decisions by sending at least one messenger. Actually less than a third of the churches are represented in conventions and only about one out of every 800 Southern Baptists take part in convention actions.

Look at the recent convention in Denver. The 13,500 messengers did not represent even one-third of the 34,000 churches in the Southern Baptist Convention. Look at one of the key votes. The 5,394 messengers who voted to recall Volume I of the Broadman Bible Commentary were a minority (about 40 percent) of the registered messengers in Denver. And so a minority of the messengers representing a minority of the churches decided a matter involving years of planning, thousands of hours of work and thousands of dollars.

This is hardly democracy. It is more demagoguery in that it encourages some with strong feelings and loud words to influence messengers in their direction. Yet it is claimed such votes are directed by the Holy Spirit and are trustworthy in determining how the majority of Southern Baptists think and feel.

Now the outcome of most convention votes may not be different if a majority of the churches were represented and all the registered messengers participated in the decision. The outcome of the vote in Denver on the commentary, for example, would likely have been the same. But this is not the point. The point is we claim the majority decided while as it works out actually the vocal minority decides.

In trying to improve our democratic process we have two alternatives. We can more properly use the present plan or we can change to another plan. The present plan seems ideal. It stresses the freedom Baptists cherish by recognizing the complete autonomy of the local congregation and the principles of voluntary cooperation. These must never be sacrificed. But if every one of the 34,000 plus churches sent its quota of messengers to the conventions, the crowd would have to move to an outdoor stadium and think of trying to conduct a business meeting with 50,000 or 60,000 messengers.

A more practical plan is some kind of delegate or representative system for conducting Southern Baptist business. It would not be too difficult to come up with a plan allowing each state to be represented in proportion to the number of Baptists in the state. The carefully chosen delegates could meet to do business. The key issues under consideration could be discussed in the local churches prior to the convention and their positions made known to the delegates through the delegates would not necessarily be instructed how to vote.

This kind of representation for Southern Baptists won't come soon. A motion approved in the 1969 convention for the Southern Baptist Executive Committee to study the problem of representation hasn't generated much interest and things will have to get much worse before we give up the ancient and cherished practice of giving every local congregation the right to be represented in conventions. Here's one Baptist who would rue the day that right is taken from every church, but it might have to be done if our conventions continue to become more demagogic than democratic.

Here is one specific suggestion for making conventions more democratic under the present plan of representation. Let more churches send messengers and let more laymen be selected as messengers. It seems in recent years too many satisfied Baptists assume the right decisions will be made at the conventions and just don't bother to go. This kind of default discourages democracy and plays into the hands of those who go to conventions determined to rule or ruin.

Actually to realize the goal of Baptist democracy our attitude is more important than any plan of representation for conventions. No plan can prevent chaos, confusion and bitterness if attitudes are bad. On the other hand Baptists who sincerely love and respect one another can practice democracy with most any plan. And so while looking for a better plan let us pray for a better spirit. (July 11, 1970)

BAPTIST UNITY WITHIN SOME DOCTRINAL DIVERSITY

THERE IS NO DOUBT THAT THE NO. 1 SOUTHERN Baptist story of 1970 was doctrinal polarization as indicated by a poll of the 30 state Baptist editors. Anyone reading Baptist publications lately or who was in Denver for the 1970 Southern Baptist Convention could not but be convinced and concerned about this polarization. Incidentally, polarization is but a big word meaning Southern Baptists are becoming more and more divided over doctrinal issues.

A persistent question for several years now has been will Southern Baptists split over some of these differences. It's a serious question because in many ways a major split would be disastrous for Southern Baptists. It would play havoc with our worldwide missionary ministry as well as injure if not actually put an end to some of our valuable agencies and institutions.

There is no need for Southern Baptists to split, at least at this time over doctrinal differences. Our differences are not that great. We should stop talking about it and quit accusing one another. We should major on accepting one another with our minor differences, loving one another and getting on with our God-given assignment of sharing Jesus Christ with all the world.

We don't have to be peas in the same pod to live together and to work together as Baptists. We can be agreed on the essentials of the divine revelation without signing one another's personal doctrinal statement. There is room for differences in interpretation without name-calling and without divorce.

Let's look at one illustration. One of the chief current doctrinal debates among Southern Baptists today is over how to interpret the Bible. The biggest disagreement is over literal and non-literal interpretations. The truth is that both the literalists and the non-literalists can accept the Bible as divinely inspired as the sole authority for our faith and practice.

For example, what does the Hebrew word for day in Genesis 1 really mean? Is it a 24-hour day or is it an indefinite period of time? The Hebrew word can mean either and is used some places in the Old Testament to mean a literal 24-hour day and elsewhere to mean an unlimited period.

Yet some Baptists insist that Genesis 1 says God created everything in its present form in six 24-hour days. By further calculation they conclude the world is about 6,000 years old.

Other Baptists considering what appears to be valid scientific evidence conclude that Genesis 1 is speaking of six eras of time and conclude that the world may be millions of years old.

What difference does it make? To debate how old the world is and to accept or reject each over a literal or non-literal view of Genesis 1 is foolish and plays into the hands of Satan who would like nothing more than to see Southern Baptists split and lose the strength of their worldwide witness.

Let those who believe in a six 24-hour day interpretation of Genesis 1 have it that way. On the other hand, let those who can take Genesis 1 into a geology or science class and show there is no basic conflict between the biblical account of creation and the most valid scientific views do so. Both interpreters can still agree on the most important message of Genesis 1. This is that no matter how or how long it was, all that was created was created by God, including man made in his image.

This does not mean that any interpretation of the Bible goes and that whatever one believes as a Baptist is all right. The letters of John which we are using for our 1971 special Bible study make this clear. The beloved apostle was concerned over false though apparently sincere teachers in the churches and proceeded to set them straight.

John insisted there was an authentic witness to the true revelation of God and that one can deny the truth by trying to make the revelation of God acceptable to the current philosophical and scientific views.

For Baptists this revelation of God's truth has been reliably put in writing by men inspired by God. This makes the Holy Scriptures trustworthy for us whether we are literalists or non-literalists. This puts us in the same fellowship and upon the same mountain. One Baptist may live on one side of the mountain while another lives on the other side, but both can live on the mountain without trying to throw each other off.

After all, it is doubtful if any Baptist has attained the peak of the mountain or has a direct pipeline to God's infallibility. Therefore humility and respect for one who differs with us are becoming for all who share the basic distinctions which have characterized Baptists through the centuries. Two of these distinctives are freedom and the belief that the Holy Spirit is available to every child of God to interpret the Bible. (January 23, 1971)

THE YEAR OF OPPORTUNITY FOR
SOUTHERN BAPTISTS

NINETEEN SEVENTY-SEVEN WILL BE REMEMBERED as the year of opportunity for Southern Baptists. Whether the future sees success or failure in ambitious undertakings, the 1977 convention in Kansas City presented Southern Baptists one of their greatest, if not their greatest, opportunity to take the gospel to every living soul on earth in this generation.

Denominational leadership received a dramatic assist from the most famous Southern Baptist of our day when United States President Jimmy Carter challenged fellow Southern Baptists to immediately put another 5,000 missionaries on mission fields of the world.

Using the theme Bold Mission Thrust, Southern Baptist leadership has been attempting to engage the masses of Baptist local church members in all-out efforts to evangelize and congregationalize every person in the world by A.D. 2000. The results of these efforts have not been too encouraging until now.

Layman Carter challenged the Kansas City convention messengers by a videotape appearance following an exciting program presentation in which messengers in Kansas City and Baptist missionaries in Hong Kong joined in an around-the-world prayer meeting by bouncing each other's messages off a satellite hundreds of miles above the earth. It was 8:35 p.m. in Kansas City and 9:35 a.m. the next day in Hong Kong. Convention messengers were amazed by this demonstration of modern communication ability of proclaiming the gospel to every corner of the earth at the same moment.

President Carter's participation in the convention was a last-moment injection. It grew out of a luncheon at the White House as recently as June 7 when layman Carter shared his dream with several key leaders of the convention. His idea of 5,000 volunteer missionaries giving at least two years of their lives to missionary service by 1982 caught on like wildfire. It bypassed ordinarily long planning channels for ideas to become official recommendations to convention messengers.

Not only is the idea exciting but that such spontaneity is still possible in the organizational structure of a 13-million member denomination is reassuring. As a veteran observer and participant in Southern Baptist life, I would have said such an idea could not have bypassed established channels and won approval.

The prayers of Southern Baptists for an open door to world evangelization in this generation have been amazingly answered. A Baptist deacon, unknown beyond his own community a few years ago but now living in the White House, has been used of God to give Southern Baptists their greatest visibility and opportunity in history. If we do not capitalize on this opportunity, we do not deserve another.

A refreshing wind of God's spirit stirred Baptists in Kansas City with renewed zeal and commitment. Pray God that it will be felt in every congregation in the land and that denominational machinery will not stifle it.

An editorial on church-state implications of President Carter's participation in the Southern Baptist Convention will appear in a coming issue of *Western Recorder*. (June 23, 1977)

ON THE PROPER WORDS TO USE

IT IS ALMOST IMPOSSIBLE TO OVERESTIMATE THE importance of communication among Baptists. Love is the tie that binds up, but clear communication is necessary for us to know one another enough to love and trust one another.

Words are our chief tools of communication, but words are tricky. They mean one thing to one person and another thing to another person. They mean one thing in one part of the country and another in other sections.

In Baptist life we usually inherit words from our predecessors and begin using them without examining their exact meaning.

One outstanding and influential religious leader in an area often influences the Baptist vocabulary for generations to come in that area.

Here are some Baptist terms that are often misleading. The term "the Baptist Church" is loosely used by some Baptists and by more non-Baptists to refer to the denomination of Baptists. There is no such thing. There is "a Baptist church" and there are "Baptist churches" but no "the Baptist Church." Some other denominations regard all local congregations as forming "the church" but not Baptists. Each Baptist church is a separate entity and completely autonomous. It volunteers to associate and cooperate with associations and conventions of churches but never regards itself as part of "the Baptist Church."

The term "delegate" is misused by some Baptists. Baptist churches do not send "delegates" to a convention or association. They send "messengers." Delegates are representatives who are instructed or delegated to express the official viewpoint of a group. Ordinarily Baptist churches do not instruct their messengers how to vote on issues but leave them to express their views under the direction of the Holy Spirit. The position expressed by a messenger doesn't bind the church he comes from but only represents his own view.

Another misuse of words is to refer to the Lord's Supper as "sacrament" or "communion." The Lord's Supper is sacred but it is not a sacrament in the church history understanding of the word. The Roman Catholics have seven sacraments, all of which are involved in a person's salvation. Each true Catholic depends on six of these sacraments for salvation (marriage and ordination are two of the seven and no true Catholic can choose both).

Baptists have no sacraments. We have two ordinances, baptism and the Lord's supper, but neither of these has any saving power. Our salvation is in the grace of God in Jesus Christ and comes to each freely and not because of any human work. Even faith by which grace is received is a gift of God.

Communion in its sweetest form is involved in proper observance of the Lord's Supper but the ordinance is better described as the Lord's Supper instead of communion.

Finally, church offerings are sometimes referred to as "dues." This is not as common now as it was in past days. Baptist churches do not assess members as do some churches of other denominations. Rather each Baptist is left to decide his own level of material giving in the light of biblical teaching and the leadership of the Holy Spirit. The intensity and pressure of some Baptist churches' stewardship campaigns come close to an assessment, but there is little danger any Baptist will hurt himself in giving under any kind of pressure.

Our contributions are tithes and offerings, not "dues."

The independence of Baptists will never allow for a common vocabulary and uniformity on interpretation of words. This is not necessary nor needful, but the use of proper words to describe universal practices would be helpful. (February 26, 1976)

A BAPTIST DAY OF ATONEMENT IS DESPERATELY NEEDED

THE CLIMAX OF THE HEBREW WORSHIP SYSTEM described in the Old Testament was the annual Day of Atonement. Once a year everybody and everything were cleansed of sin in order to begin a new year with the approval and blessings of Jehovah.

On this one day of each year the high priest exchanged his priestly robes for a simple white tunic. He first entered the Holy of Holies with blood to be sprinkled before the mercy seat seeking forgiveness for his own sins and the sins of his fellow priests. Then all areas of the tabernacle or the temple used for worship along with all the other worship paraphernalia were cleansed. Finally the sins of all the people were put upon the head of the scapegoat who bore them away to the wilderness. The people were then filled with joy for forgiveness and restoration of fellowship with Jehovah.

This ancient Hebrew ceremony speaks to our needs today. Not in its ritualistic details but in its true meaning. We need a Baptist Day of Atonement like we need nothing else.

To put it in more familiar words, we need a denominational revival. Like the Day of Atonement it should begin at the top and continue until it includes everything and everybody. Everything about our Baptist program as well as everyone of us should fall prostrate before the mercy seat of God for cleansing and renewal.

What are the sins which so easily beset Baptists and for which we must repent and be forgiven in order to experience the approval of God? They're not always easy to see and they are even harder to admit. We had rather rationalize than to reason and to be judged by our own or the world's standards rather than by God's searching word.

There is the deadly sin of presumption and pride both as a denomination and as persons. We have taken the manifold blessings of God upon Baptists as a guarantee of his full approval rather than as a privilege which must be matched with responsibility. We tend to think we have a corner on truth and have a perfect understanding of God's revelations. What presumption! We have even shouted that Baptists are the one hope of God for the world instead of confessing that God is the one hope for Baptists.

There is the sin of loving this present world and what it offers. With rare exceptions Baptists today are all—pastors and denominational leaders and workers included—caught up in the American craze of things and the religion of materialism. Many Baptists spend more on one house to live in or one car to ride in than they give to God and his work in their whole lifetime. Even the minister gets caught up on this status-minded culture and has to dress, live and otherwise receive and spend what the world counts proper for his position.

We preach the gospel of One who did not have the earthly security of the foxes and the birds, and we profess to follow him who had no place to lay his head, but we often deliver our sermons in luxurious sanctuaries to those at ease in Zion walking on carpeted floors and sitting on cushioned pews. We ride to the church in air conditioned machines from mortgaged homes filled with latest antiques to talk about the crosses we bear. All the time we see to it that our pastor has a new car, a boat or a cabin on the lake because somehow it makes us feel a little better about ours.

Probably the most damaging sin of all among Baptists in the Lord's sight is our choice of self over others and the absence of genuine love for each other. Too many pastors distrust their members and use them for selfish ends. Criticism of the pastor and cutting him to pieces are favorite sports of many church members.

When the chips are down in the controversial issues in the church, the pastor is often deserted though he is right because the members think more of each other and their mutual approval in the days ahead than they do for the principle of right.

As preachers we say all kinds of extravagantly complimentary things about each other in public but what we really think of each other is another thing. We use one another for personal advantage and most of us have never shed a sympathizing tear for each other. We distrust each other and are among the last to forgive one another.

Pastors and denominational leaders sometimes act as if theirs is the only work of the Lord. We push and shove to get our own little kingdoms and then make ourselves immune to any questioning by declaring we have a direct word from the Lord. We put the sanction of God on everything we do as if our will must always be his will.

I am aware that this all sounds negative and unduly critical. I also know all is not bad about us, but as I examine my own soul and observe my fellow Baptists, I can but conclude there is a deep spiritual sickness upon us. Furthermore, this will be a sickness unto death unless we admit our malady and accept the surgery of the Great Physician.

The kind of Baptist revival we need is not the traditional type producing momentary repentance and resumption of our old ways. We need to be rocked from stem to stern and shaken from top to bottom by the devastating judgment of God and remade by the creative power of the living Lord never to be the same again.

This is the Baptist Day of Atonement so desperately needed. Who will join this sinner for such a cleansing? (September 8, 1966)

APPRECIATING OUR BAPTIST HERITAGE

LACK OF APPRECIATION BY SOME CHURCHES FOR their Southern Baptist heritage is shameful. It is important that churches know something of their roots and not treat lightly their heritage.

This is not to say everything in our past is of God. The practice and defense of slavery which figured prominently in the organization of the Southern Baptist Convention were surely not divinely inspired, but God surely was in Southern Baptist beginnings in spite of our shortcomings.

That scattered groups of Baptists with wide doctrinal differences and suspicion of one another ever got together as a denomination is almost unbelievable. Only the work of Almighty God could accomplish it.

What has come of the humble beginnings of Southern Baptist theological education in 1859 and of the establishment of a controversial publishing house (Sunday School Board) is a sure sign of the Lord's approval.

The result now is that individual Baptists and Baptist churches have as much or more valuable resources to draw upon than any believers and churches in America. There is no place for boasting except in the Lord but we are envied by many other church groups in America.

We should never take for granted nor underrate this heritage. Everyone who reads this page regularly knows I am not a blind denominational loyalist but every day I live I cherish true Baptist heritage more and more and I tend to become more and more intolerant of those who disregard or abuse this valuable asset.

A large majority of Southern Baptist churches appreciate and depend upon denominational resources to help them accomplish their divine mission. They depend upon denominational help for church music and religious educational materials, for all building suggestions, for stewardship plans and materials, for theological training of staff members, for national and worldwide missionary programs through which to channel their mission gifts and for many other needs. They realize their efforts would be severely curtailed without this cooperative relationship.

But in recent years a few Southern Baptist churches have seemed to have outgrown their need for and appreciation of their denominational connection. They have become super churches with enough financial and human resources to do all the things alone which they once did with fellow Baptist churches. They organize their own missionary journeys, spending huge sums to send witnessing teams, choirs and staff members to other areas of America and even to foreign lands. Some produce some, if not all, of their own literature and educational materials. They start their own elementary and high schools, Bible colleges and even theological schools to teach their own interpretation of the scriptures.

Actually they become more like little separate denominations than the great Southern Baptist cooperating churches they once were. They still belong to the state and national conventions and contribute to Southern Baptist causes but in declining proportion to the magnitude of their own programs.

Much of this is admirable. Local church direct involvement in evangelistic and missionary projects at home and even abroad stimulates even more evangelistic and missionary zeal in a congregation. Creative church music and religious educational programs by local church staff members are to be expected.

But there is a limit. Organizing grandiose evangelistic and missionary projects and starting schools to perpetuate one man's interpretation of scripture and theological positions can but say these church leaders believe other Baptist schools and denominational missionary efforts are not doing the job.

We are accustomed to thinking of this being done by preachers like Jerry Falwell, Bob Jones and Oral Roberts. They are independents who have set out to make and perpetuate their own heritage. Their movements are largely personality oriented and their successors probably will not be able to advance or even maintain the movements.

The Southern Baptist heritage is far more than this and we should never forget the rock from which we are hewn. (March 4, 1981)

THE MAKING OF MISSIONARIES

IN AN UNUSUAL SPIRIT OF CONSECRATION THE words of the hymn "Where He Leads Me" were being sung. An invitation had been given and everyone present sensed the presence and power of the Holy Spirit. God was at work. Hearts were hearing his voice and wills were surrendering to his call.

The scene was the Southern Baptist Seminary chapel and the occasion was Missionary Day. It was May 1, 1958, and the usual activities of the day had reached a climax in the chapel where hundreds of God's called were assembled. Standing in the front were two couples who were missionary volunteers. Both these couples had been in Kingdom work in Kentucky pastorates but would soon be saying goodbye to friends and loved ones in this part of the world to serve God in other places of the earth. The

James McKinleys would be sailing soon to far away Pakistan in Asia and the Hugh McKinleys would be in Spain on another continent.

Behind the pulpit stood Missionary Tommy Halsell, recently returned on furlough from Brazil. Following the moving testimonies of the new missionaries, Tommy had laid bare his heart with all of its compassion and consecration. I was in the service because Tommy was the speaker. We were classmates at the seminary. Several years ago I had visited the church in Memphis where Tommy was pastor. I sensed there the warmth of the fellowship. I felt the love of his people for him and was amazed at the influence of his life among his young people. Tommy was a brilliant, young, dynamic pastor. His name would be in the hands of pulpit committees from the most attractive Baptist churches, humanly speaking.

But something happened to Tommy which he told about in this Missionary Day service. Not by any sudden illumination nor by any mystic experience but in a very normal way truths which he had never seriously reflected upon began to invade his soul. He began to become disturbingly aware of the great expanses of the world without a witness of the good news of God in Christ. His heart was sorely troubled as he was made to realize that there were 23,000 Southern Baptist preachers for the 70 million people who lived in Southern Baptist territory while there were less than 300 Southern Baptist preachers witnessing to the other billions and millions of the earth. True we had more than 300 foreign missionaries, but the majority then as now were women.

About this same time the former schoolmates of Tommy visited him from the mission field and enlisted his prayers for the needs of so many large areas of Brazil without a true witness of Christ. Tommy did the dangerous thing of praying and learned that the answer to his prayer was his own life. In a few months he found himself in South America with his wife, whose life had been placed beside his.

Now the invitation was being given for others to place their lives on the altar of mission service. One after another quietly moved into the aisles and down the front until a row stretched out across the front of the chapel. In all 17 came. Among these were three married couples. In the arms of one father with head nestled on his shoulder was a little child sleeping through this moment that meant many things for the child. It might mean being reared in a distant land with strangely colored playmates far from the comforts and pleasures of America. It would likely mean separation from parents in order to find education and training. But most of all it meant being the child of parents in God's will. What a nap! I found tears in my own eyes as I wondered if I should not have traveled this aisle years ago.

To me this was a great moment for God among Baptists. I thought of other great moments in Baptist history. I thought of that day in England when William Carey pled for the earth's millions while a fellow Baptist preacher said, "Sit down, Mr. Carey! When God is ready to save the heathen, he will save them without any help from you or me." I remembered also that eventful day when two missionaries on their way from America to a mission field under the auspices of another denomination made a serious study of the New Testament and discovered they were Baptists. But Baptists had little missionary concern and no mission boards to appoint and support missionaries. One of the two, Adoniram Judson, went on the field while the other, Luther Rice, returned to America to fan the mission flames in Baptists. The names of Judson and Rice are emblazoned on seminary apartment buildings that stand hard by the chapel and what was happening in this Missionary Day service in 1958 would have set the hearts of these early missionaries to singing.

I rejoiced at what God had wrought among Baptists since the days of Carey, Judson and Rice. As we pass the 1,200 mark we are planning definitely for 1,800 missionaries by 1964. From a denomination of no schools and no missionaries not so long ago, as time is counted, we are humbled at God's grace as we count our seminaries with 5,000 young men and women training for God's service, our 51 Baptist colleges plus institutes and academies with over 55,000 students, more than 8,000 of whom are training for the ministry of preaching, education or music. In our seminaries more than 900 men and women are mission volunteers and in our colleges 1,325 young people have already said they will go where God leads them.

It's a great day to be alive. It's a great day to be a Baptist. God is making missionaries by calling young people and by leading Baptists every time an offering envelope is prepared. (May 15, 1958)

FIRST, THEN AND ALWAYS

GODLY WOMEN WERE THE FIRST TO DISCOVER the glorious empty tomb on the first Easter morning, and a woman was the first person to whom Christ appeared. Ever since then, women have been first in love, devotion and service to Christ and his church.

This is seen nowhere more clearly than in the Woman's Missionary Union movement among Southern Baptist women. The 75th anniversary of this noble organization is being celebrated this year with due honor. In Kentucky, Baptist women consistently lead the way and put the rest of us to shame. This is demonstrated in many local churches and is overwhelmingly evident each year when the ladies gather for their Woman's Missionary Union convention.

Last year, when the ladies met at Crescent Hill Baptist Church in Louisville, seats were all taken long before each session began. Again this year the historic First Church auditorium in Lexington was filled beyond capacity.

How are such interest and attendance accounted for in a time when lack of attendance at other Baptist meetings is of growing concern? Several reasons come to mind. Obviously such success cannot be explained apart from able and faithful leadership like that of our Kentucky Baptist WMU Executive Secretary, Mrs. George Fergerson, and her staff. Add to these such dynamic personalities as Mrs. J.S. Woodward, only to mention one of the state officers, and the explanation is easy.

Another reason for the popularity of WMU conventions is the outstanding program always planned. One inspirational feature after another is bright contrast with some Baptist gatherings. But there is one explanation above all others. This is the high quality of dedication and commitment on the part of thousands of Baptist women in Kentucky. We might as well face it—the women outshine the men when it comes to the Lord's work. If the men's work has its thousands, the women's work has its tens of thousands. Whether innately or not, Baptist women are more religious than Baptist men and find more ways to express their love for Jesus Christ. The far-reaching influence of these godly women can never be measured by human standards. How many young people have been turned to the Lord and his service by faithful WMU women will never be known this side of glory.

A person is fortunate who can remember as many as a half dozen persons who had profound influence upon him in days of youth. Of those in my own memory as a lad, three women are high on the list. These were my mother, one school teacher and a wonderful lady who for many years was "Mrs. WMU" of our association. My mother was WMU president for many years in our little church and took me as a Sunbeam and Royal Ambassador many times to associational WMU meetings to say little pieces. I cannot separate my call to the ministry from these experiences when first the Lord seemed to be calling me to preach his gospel.

In my own mind I still question the wisdom of transferring Royal Ambassador work a few years ago to the men of our Baptist churches. Though it stands to reason that boys' work rightly belongs to the men, our performance in many instances has not justified the trust placed in us. The dedication and perseverance of women who worked with Royal Ambassadors more than offset any natural disadvantages.

In searching for explanations for the decline among Southern Baptists in recent years of the number of young men giving themselves to the ministry and church-related vocations, is it not possible here is an overlooked explanation. In calling out the called, neither the preacher nor the brothers may be quite as effective as the ladies of the WMU.

Considering the low estate of women in the ancient world and recalling the ministry of our Lord in lifting women to their intended place, it is clear, no one ever did so much for women as Jesus. Recalling Southern Baptist history and the first 75 years of WMU, it is clear none of us ever did so much for Christ and the mission cause as have our women. Their devotion to Christ and the mission cause among Southern Baptists make for one of the brightest hopes for the next 75 years of Southern Baptist history. (April 18, 1963)

WHAT ABOUT SUNDAY NIGHTS FOR BAPTISTS?

WILL BAPTIST CHURCHES SOON BE DARK ON Sunday nights with evening training and worship activities only a memory for the past? Is Training Union already dead except for a gasp here and there? Should people who get up to attend morning worship and even Sunday School be expected to come back on Sunday night? Isn't one worship service on Sunday enough? These and similar questions are often asked over coffee cups by Baptists though they are rarely raised in business meetings or discussed officially in church committees.

An honest answer to the first question is that at the present rate of decline in Sunday night attendance more and more Baptist churches will follow the example of many congregations of other denominations in calling off Sunday night activities. There are notable exceptions but Sunday night is an embarrassing sight in many Baptist churches.

Our first tendency is to bemoan the spiritual decline of this age and talk about our fellow Baptists who have deserted the Lord's house for some place or activity of their choosing. We wish for the good old days when the Sunday night crowd often outnumbered the morning congregation and Church Training was not far behind Sunday School in attendance. We are certain we could have these again if only Baptists were not so spiritually cold.

It is not that simple, however. We forget that in the lifetime of many of us society has changed from basically agricultural and rural to industrial and urban. In the good old days the church was about the only place to go and it served a social and even a recreational need as well as a spiritual one. Today's affluence has given many church members trailers, boats, cabins on the lake and other recreational equipment which they never had before. The countryside and even small towns have been largely emptied of young adults who have gone to cities for employment as machines more and more replaced them on the farm. Modern technology has provided many enjoyable things like color television which in turn has contributed to the professional football mania whose weekly cultic activities often coincide with the Church Training period on Sunday evening. In addition to all this is the stealing of the Lord's Day by greedy businesses which require employees to work during regular worship hours and which tempt Sunday shoppers with super specials. Many of these business shrines begin their Sunday services at 11 a.m., the same hour historically reserved for morning worship.

Taking note of what's happening on Sunday nights, Southern Baptist Church Training leaders have launched a "save Sunday night for worship, training and fellowship" effort. With the slogan, "Church—the Sunday Night Place," a noble effort is being made to stem the Sunday night decline. Thanks to these for their concern and efforts.

But neither denominational promotion nor brow-beating of members by pastors will get it done. Unusual gimmicks including contests and spectaculars of many kinds are a temporary boost but are generally short-lived and often leave the patient worse off than before.

How a church member spends Sunday and Sunday night is a revelation of the extent of his Christian commitment and spiritual depth. It is not that God is a scorekeeper putting stars by our names for every time we go to the church, but if we truly love the Lord we will long for the special day and special place to meet him and our spiritual brothers and sisters.

A popular and growing view among Baptists is that we can do anything we please on Sunday after we have gone to church. And so we like the early service, especially in summer, because we can get our obligation to God over and have for ourselves the rest of the day. Drive-in early worship services in beach attire, with trailer hooked up and an itch to get going are growing in popularity.

What does this say? Actually it says Sunday is ours and we favor God by giving him a little bit of it. It's like pinching off a little piece of candy to give to the one whose it actually is while keeping the bar for ourselves. Sunday is the Lord's, not ours. How much of it is to be spent in specific worship, learning and training activities is up to him. Sunday night is still Sunday. If the Lord wants Sunday mornings and Sunday nights, he has a perfect right to them as well as all the time between.

When it comes to Sunday night in Baptist churches, it is not a matter of saving the Church Training hour and the traditional evening hour. It is a matter of saving ourselves from spiritual starvation, a fruitless life without training and a woeful accounting to God for taking for our fleshly gratification what he has provided for our spiritual renewal. (September 23, 1972)

CRITICISM WITHOUT CONFIDENCE CAN
BE TOO DESTRUCTIVE

THE SPIRIT OF REVOLT OF OUR DAY IS BREAKING
up ancient and revered social, political and religious structures. The control of many homes has already passed from
parents to the children. Long established racial structures in
America and all over the world have been toppled, and even old
religious structures like Roman Catholicism are reeling from
revolution.

All religious structures probably need the benefits of criticism
but the danger always is the good will be thrown away with the
bad. Whatever happens to Roman Catholicism in this age of
revolt, let us be careful about what happens to Southern Baptists.
Some purging we always need, but let us not start a fire that will
consume the good with the bad.

Churches and denominations have become favorite whipping
boys in our day. There is hardly a good word for Baptist churches
and the Southern Baptist Convention today except from those
regarded as naive and without discernment. It is high time
responsible observers spoke up for the preservation of much we
have as Baptists.

If Baptists benefit from this spirit of criticism without letting it
destroy much that is good, there is one characteristic we must
embrace and strengthen. This is the spirit of confidence and trust in
each other. This is not to advocate blind confidence and uncondi-
tional trust but confidence and trust that become fellow Christians.

The need for mutual confidence is in every area of Baptist life
today. In interpreting the Bible, for example, the Baptist scholar
and layman must trust each other. They need each other in
finding the best understanding of the revelation of God. The
temptation always is for the layman to suspect the scholar of
trying to undermine the Bible and for the scholar to look with
contempt upon the untutored layman.

The same goes for the pastor and the congregation. In too many churches the mutual confidence with which the pastor and congregation began is soon lost and it becomes pastor versus congregation and congregation versus pastor. The pastor loses confidence in an apathetic and critical congregation and the congregation uses roast preacher as a regular diet.

Even denominational leadership and pastors encounter the same problem. Somehow the Baptist Building man is regarded too often as only a clever manipulator and the denominational worker at times feels the pastor is too protective of his congregation and unresponsive to world needs.

The three paragraphs above overstate the case for the sake of emphasis but the problem justifies such emphasis. Let us be done with such unchristian attitudes.

Jesus thought and expected the best of his humanly weak disciples, and they were the better for his confidence. We can help each other by trusting others like Jesus did. It is better to believe the best about others and be disappointed should they fail than to believe the worst about others and brag on our insight when they fail. (August 8, 1968)

IT HAS NOT ALWAYS BEEN EASY TO BE A BAPTIST

THE SUCCESS AND STRENGTH OF BAPTISTS IN America today tend to make for presumption, apathy and lack of appreciation for the sacrifices and suffering of early Baptists in the new world. We presume Baptists have always been free and influential. Not so! The religious freedom and other advantages we enjoy today did not come easily but were earned at a high price.

Baptists in many communities of America today not only are free to worship as they please but also enjoy prestige and influence. In the Southern United States, or the Bible Belt as it is

called, Baptists outnumber any other religious group. The
majority of professional and business men also are Baptists and
so are the local political office holders.

Membership in a Baptist church in such areas has become a
status symbol. Ambitious businessmen and public office candidates find it advantageous to be Baptists. Thus Baptists today
occupy the kind of favored position enjoyed by Episcopalians in
colonial Virginia and Congregationalists in early Massachusetts.

Baptist church membership in such situations tends to lose its
true meaning. Generally those things which cost little mean little.
It is easier to be a Baptist than not to be in such communities, and
the cost is in not being instead of being a Baptist. From the beginning it was not so. Maybe one requirement for Baptist church
membership should be a study of early Baptists in England, on
the continent and in early America.

The first Baptists in America came from England and were
seeking freedom from harassment and harsh treatment. But in
those days Baptists were poor and passage across the Atlantic
was expensive. The cost of crossing was equal to about two years
wages and very likely the only way some Baptists could finance
the trip was to sell themselves to indentured servitude.

But even for those with the fare it was a hazardous trip. The
church historian J. Davis tells of the trials of Abel Morgan and
his family in reaching the new world. The ship set sail September
28, 1710. On the second day the wind turned against them
forcing the ship to pull into a port and wait three weeks before
trying again. But the winds again opposed them and they were
forced to wait another five weeks in an Irish port.

By then many of the passengers were ill, including the
Morgan family, but the voyage was resumed. On December 14
Morgan's little boy died and three days later his wife passed
away. Both were buried at sea and Morgan finally arrived in
America on February 14, 1711, four and a half months after
setting sail.

Nor did Baptists always find a haven of religious freedom in the new world. They were among the dissenters expelled from the Massachusetts Bay Colony. In Virginia they even fared worse. There the Church of England was the established church and everyone was required to recognize it. A license from the state was required to preach, and licenses were often denied Baptists or Baptist preachers went ahead preaching without seeking licenses. Baptists were harassed for refusing to let their children be baptized as infants and insisting upon immersion for baptism. In many ways these early Virginia Baptists were second-class citizens.

Legal persecution and prosecution were common in Virginia in the 1760s and 1770s. Five Baptist preachers were arrested in 1768 and spent 43 days in jail. In 1771 a magistrate and the official parish clergyman invaded a Baptist worship service, throwing the preacher and five of his fellow Baptist preachers in jail. Some were whipped and all were commanded not to preach any more. They refused to obey and preached through the windows of the jail. The records reveal that more than 30 Baptist preachers in at least nine Virginia counties were jailed during the era.

These obstinate Baptists and their insistence upon complete religious freedom were part of the inspiration of men like Patrick Henry and James Madison in demanding the freedom which was eventually guaranteed by the inclusion of the Bill of Rights in the United States Constitution. In the 200 years since the persecution of Baptists the scene has completely changed. Baptists today in many places occupy the same kind of prominence and power the Episcopalians enjoyed in early Virginia though without legal sanction.

But ease and commitment are not always compatible. Today a Baptist church is one of the easiest things to get into and the hardest to get out of. Maybe just the reverse ought to be so. A Baptist church should be one of the hardest things to get into and easy to get out of. (August 24, 1974)

DALEY OBSERVATIONS ON ISSUES OF THE DAY

WESTERN RECORDER

VOLUNTARY PRAYER IN PUBLIC SCHOOLS IS ALREADY LEGAL

AFTER ALREADY BEGINNING ANOTHER EDITORIAL for this issue, a telephone call from a highly respected Kentucky Baptist pastor leads me to try to clarify further widespread misunderstanding about the present status of Bible reading and prayer in public schools and what the 1962 and 1963 Supreme Court decisions allow and disallow in the way of religious activities in public schools.

The editor's mail and this pastor's call indicate where the problem lies and why there is such strong sentiment for the "prayer amendment." So many responses to this editor's assurance that voluntary prayer and Bible reading were not ruled out by the Supreme Court's decisions say that no matter what the decisions said or the editor claims, the actual result was complete elimination of Bible reading and prayer in all our public schools.

What is the explanation? To begin with, the claim that Bible reading and prayer have been completely eliminated from public schools is not true. Voluntary Bible reading and prayer by individual students and even by teachers go on in many public schools every day and is completely legal so long as it is not officially sponsored, planned or conducted by school officials or teachers.

On the other hand it has been claimed, without verification so far, that some school officials have made a blanket ruling against all kinds of prayer and Bible reading, voluntary, private or otherwise. If so, the school officials are wrong and should be appealed to for correction of this policy or taken to court.

Why have some school officials been inclined to outcourt the Supreme Court, so to speak? There are probably two main reasons. The first is that it is easier just to adopt a blanket policy of no prayer and Bible reading than to try to determine what is and what isn't legal and become involved in endless controversy and discussion over the matter. The second reason is that too many teachers have proceeded to ignore the Supreme Court rulings and have continued to conduct religious services of one kind or another in their classrooms. No matter how well meaning they are, they are breaking the law in doing this and have to be stopped by school officials.

Once more let's understand what the Supreme Court said. It said that the First Amendment puts the state out of religious affairs except to say no religion can be officially sponsored by law and no law can be passed to prevent anyone from freely exercising his right to worship. To put it another way, the First Amendment says religion is outside the province of the authority of the state. This is why a school teacher who is a public employee paid with tax funds cannot legally conduct or sponsor religious services during school hours. Before or after school she or he can teach the Bible, lead prayer meetings, preach sermons, conduct revivals or engage in any other religious activity with the possible exception of snake handling or similar practices which endanger public welfare.

Please do this editor a favor. If anyone knows of a school where a student cannot on a voluntary basis, not only take his Bible to school but can read it during his free time or cannot bow his head and silently thank the Lord before he eats his school lunch, let me know. If this is the case, it's time for insistence upon or even legal action to claim the "free exercise" portion of the First Amendment.

This kind of an approach is far better than approving the "prayer amendment" which actually cancels the First Amendment and puts the government into the business of telling people where and what kind of praying they can do.

This "prayer amendment" is up for consideration in the House of Representatives on November 8. It's still time to contact your congressmen to express your concern for religious liberty by preserving the present language of the First Amendment without any "prayer amendment." (October 30, 1971)

YOUTH REBELLION CAN BE YOUTH REVIVAL

ONE OF THE GRAVEST DANGERS FOR CHURCHES today is the inclination to write off modern youth. Protests, demonstrations, violence and other behavior of young people today are so far from what we have considered ideal that we feel we might as well give up on them.

We had better stop and think again before we count youth out. We dare not react to the behavior of some of them with condemnation of all of them. To refer to them as "bums" without separating the good from the bad is stupid.

Without a doubt there are among today's young people some out-and-out radicals who are bent on violence, destruction and anarchy. These are dangerous and should be restrained by whatever force is necessary. Leniency to the point of permissiveness has never been the answer in dealing with youth.

Furthermore, a sizable number of idealistic young people are caught up with the extremists and sometimes searching youth are overcome by the mob spirit and participate in violence. This is characteristic of youth and it is too much to expect from them the restraint and maturity which only age and experience can bring.

Has it occurred to us that what we are seeing is a revival as well as a revolution among youth? If we stop shouting back to them long enough to listen to what they are saying, we might be surprised. We call them rebels without a cause but they have more cause than first appears.

The words heard most often from today's young people are love and peace but we cannot hear their words because of our preoccupation with the way they dress, wear their hair and behave. They may not even know the full meaning of these words but they know things are not right and they are ready to give their lives for making a better world.

Note who is involved in the aggressive youth movement. Not those who are drafted but those who volunteer. It is revealing that it is mostly not the youth from poor homes who protest poverty and go to Appalachia to help with their hands but young people from homes of affluence and wealth. It is not just the cowards who are calling for the end of the Vietnamese conflict but young people who see the folly of the slaughter of the flower of American manhood and are courageous enough to appear disloyal and unpatriotic to protest it. The Old Testament prophets and Jesus himself called for many of the same things young people are calling for today.

If we had really believed the teaching of the Bible we could have expected the present youth rebellion. God has assured us that wealth, luxury and worldly pleasure do not satisfy a man's soul. Yet we have lived and worked to give our children these things and now they are throwing them in our face and marching off in protest to live in rags and hunger sometimes.

There is no doubt about it. The objectives of the majority of today's youth are spiritual. The trouble is they are turning to unspiritual methods to achieve spiritual ends. Many of them seem to be saying, "We have good things started but we don't know how to finish them. Come on and help us."

The big question is not what will happen to them but what will happen to us. Will we be responsive enough to listen to what they are really trying to say? Will we be flexible enough to join them in working for a better world? Will we be resourceful enough to offer them spiritual means to work for spiritual goals? This is one of the crucial challenges of the churches today. What a tragedy if a true revival is going on among today's young people and the church misses out on it by not even recognizing it! (June 6, 1970)

THE BIG LIE ABOUT LIQUOR

ORDINARILY THE QUALITY OF NEWS REPORTING in the Louisville *Courier-Journal* is good but occasionally it reflects a strong bias which is unworthy of a responsible newspaper. Such is the case in a front page article in the January 14 issue.

The lengthy article dwells upon the failure of the law against legal sale of alcoholic beverages in many counties in Kentucky. The article tries to make readers believe that widespread dishonesty and corruption of public officials is due to this awful law against legal sales of liquor. Areas where sale of alcoholic beverages is legal are pictured as much better off than those where sales are illegal so far as law enforcement and honesty of public officials is concerned.

There's nothing new in this argument, but it insults the intelligence of the reader. The argument is since all illegal sales of alcoholic beverages cannot be stopped, the law against legal sale is bad and should be abolished.

Where does such logic lead? Apply it to murder. Murder is against the law but in spite of all the efforts of law enforcement officers, murders still take place and are on the increase in many communities. Does this mean since the law against murder doesn't stop all murder, it should be abolished?

The news writer quotes statistics on liquor related arrests in dry counties as proof that the liquor is illegally sold in the dry counties. No doubt some of it is but the fact is drinkers in a dry county ordinarily can easily drive a few miles and buy their drinks in a wet county.

The most absurd of all the arguments against prohibition is it corrupts local officials. The contention is that these officials cannot resist accepting payoffs and bribes in return for winking at violations of the law.

The clear answer to this argument is included in a quote from Pike County Commonwealth Attorney Paul Runyon which is included in the article. Runyon points out laws don't make officials corrupt. If they are dishonest and crooked, it will be revealed one way or another. If they are honest and straight, liquor sales laws nor anything else will corrupt them.

Advocates of legal sale of alcoholic beverages resort to every conceivable point to make prohibitionists appear dumb and blind. One of their favorite charges is that preachers and bootleggers work together to keep liquor sales illegal because it helps the causes of both. No charge could be a bigger lie.

Preachers and others who oppose legal sales of liquor are concerned about the evil effects of the product, not who profits from the sales. It's blood money whether a law-abiding citizen, the state or a bootlegger makes it selling this destructive product.

How any sane person can justify the sale of such a destructive product is hard to understand. The facts are clear. The per-capita annual consumption of alcohol is 52.5 gallons for every American over 14 years old. It is estimated lost production from alcoholism each year is $19.6 billion, cost to heath is $12.7 billion, cost in violent crime is $2.8 billion and cost in motor vehicle accidents is $5.1 billion.

Half of all the highway fatalities are due to drinking drivers, and alcoholism is the leading cause of death among persons between the ages of 15-24.

The basic explanation for the liquor industry and its defense can be put in one word—greed. It is said the gross income of the liquor industry in America is $38.2 billion a year. This figures out to $4.3 million dollars an hour. As long as it is that profitable, the liquor champions and their lies will be heard in many places, including front pages of newspapers. (January 30, 1980)

A STATE LOTTERY HAS NO PLACE IN KENTUCKY

IT'S POSSIBLE THAT THE PRESCRIPTION IS MORE deadly than the illness. This is definitely the case when a state-sponsored lottery is recommended as a cure for state revenue shortfall. The truth is the legalized lottery idea is a disease and it threatens to become an epidemic.

State-sponsored lotteries are already operating in 18 states and are being proposed in several other states at this time. Kentucky is almost certain to be one of these states facing this issue in 1984. The lottery idea was proposed, debated and defeated several years ago by the Kentucky General Assembly but the idea is not dead. The unsuccessful Republican candidate for Kentucky governor last year proposed a state lottery to benefit education and actually pre-filed a lottery bill in the General Assembly.

Kentuckians need to look carefully at any proposal for a state lottery no matter what cause is supposed to benefit from it. Good causes ought not seek support from such an immoral means as gambling.

Publicly legalized lotteries, like any other gambling, are addictive, especially with lower-income people who can least

afford to spend their limited income in hopes of getting rich
through chance.

An Associated Press release last year told the story of Richard
Smith, a 19-year-old Pennsylvanian who took his life's savings of
$6,000 and spent it all on state lottery tickets in hope of winning
the one $1 million prize. Of course, he lost it all because his
chances for winning were infinitesimally slim in spite of buying
$6,000 worth of tickets. Disappointed with losing, Richard
downed 200 aspirin tablets in a suicide attempt.

Richard's is an extreme case to be sure, but there are more
Richards resulting from lotteries than there are $1 million
winners.

In victimizing those least able to afford to gamble, lotteries
multiply the cost of welfare to care for mates and children of
addictive gamblers and to try to rehabilitate them. The cost in
human destruction far outstrips any financial benefits from
lottery gambling. Knowledgeable people see lotteries for what
they are.

Business economics professor Ross Wilhelm of the University
of Michigan says: "When state-run lotteries were first proposed,
I strongly supported them. ... I was completely wrong and naive
in taking such a position. The stark reality is that state lotteries
are among the worst rip-offs of all forms of gambling in the
nation. The viciousness of state-run games is compounded
beyond belief by the fact that state governments actively adver-
tise and promote games and the winners. It is difficult to see
much benefit to society of this means of diverting the energies
and resources of the people away from important producing
activities."

The only possible benefit from state-operated lotteries is the
financial profit and this is greatly exaggerated. In no state where
a lottery has been legalized have the financial returns been as
much as first promised. The more successful legalized lotteries
have been those in which the state has gone all-out to promote

and encourage participation. Who wants Kentucky to become an advertising agent for gambling?

As Kentuckians let us be forthright. If the best management of present tax income does not result in enough resources to provide necessary services, let's agree on a fair and equitable means to secure more revenue instead of turning to any form of gambling which victimizes humans and degrades a state.

This is a plea for every *Western Recorder* reader to contact his or her representative and senator in the Kentucky General Assembly today. Let them know you oppose a state lottery. (January 17, 1984)

HOLDING THE LINE

THE PRESENT GENERATION FACES A MULTITUDE of problems. Some of these are age-old while others have slipped in so gradually during our own generation as to be remindful of the proverbial camel who eventually took his master's entire tent after beginning with his nose inside.

Because of their constant exposure, some of these current evils are well known. The propaganda machines keep us up on communism and the pulpits warn us of atheism and materialism, but the insidious foes which overtake us unaware are our most dangerous enemies.

Every thinking person could compile a considerable list of these and a book would be required to contain them all. Not to burden you with my entire list but simply to express one of my present concerns, let me name a current danger high on my list. Moral laxity which has almost completely overtaken all of us poses a grave threat to what we have considered a decent way of life. In the realm of morals there is too much shallow thinking among us. We have two extremes. To some, almost any human activity is immoral with smoking, dancing, card playing, mixed swimming and even the use of makeup being the more deadly types of moral sins. On the other hand, others believe almost anything is all right and they practice what they believe. We should recognize that morality is founded upon the nature of God, not upon the ideas of man. What men think changes from generation to generation; what God thinks never changes. From the word of God we should construct our moral fences and hold the line right there.

Now for the sake of illustration let me mention one place where the line has given way to the quiet, gradual, insidious approach of a direct violation of God's moral law. The fourth commandment sets one day of each week apart for holy purposes. No decision of man as to how to use this day changes the intention of God for it.

There have been times in our own national history when we held rather rigidly to the biblical teaching. By law man was prohibited from much activity of any kind on the Lord's Day. New England records show a sea captain returning on Sunday from a long voyage was fined for kissing his wife on the Lord's Day. I doubt if this has much biblical support or the Lord's sanction, but it serves to show how we have changed.

Nowadays anything done any other day is done on Sunday and some things are deliberately put off until then. Lawnmowers, washing machines, sweepers and even tractors often work overtime on God's time. Their sound has become so familiar as to be accepted by man, but those who so desecrate the Lord's Day must expect to answer to a God who said, "Remember the Sabbath day, to keep it holy." It all began when drug stores and other essential services were made available on Sunday. Who could argue against this? Jesus approved doing good on the Sabbath. But it continued with service stations, delicatessens, etc., and now has come to used car lots, grocery stores, etc. Somewhere we passed over the line separating necessary and helpful services to unnecessary and selfish indulgence.

It began with families using Sunday for visiting friends and relatives and soon very bold sinners played golf or went fishing on Sunday. Now it's an exodus to playgrounds, lakes, golf courses, etc., on Sunday. First the known sinner, then an uncommitted church member and last Sunday afternoon a deacon going up the lake in his boat chanced to meet his preacher coming down the lake in his boat.

It's time we go back and find that line and finding it, to hold it. Where were you last Sunday? In Sunday school? Good, then cut this out and slip it under the door of your neighbor who went to the lake. I'll give him one later to slip under yours. (August 14, 1958)

MORE ON THE TEN COMMANDMENTS IN PUBLIC SCHOOLS

THE VIEWS OF THE KENTUCKY BAPTIST CONvention public affairs committee on House Bill 156 calling for the posting of the Ten Commandments in public school classrooms reported in the February 7 issue of *Western Recorder* has brought a deluge of protesting letters. The volume of letters was intensified by suggestions by some champions of this project that expressions be sent to Executive Secretary Frank Owen and to this editor.

Responses to *Western Recorder* news articles and editorials are always welcome and generally acknowledged personally by the editor. In this instance the volume of mail is now such that we simply cannot answer each letter individually. I had not planned to editorialize further on this issue but feel I must now do so in light of the numerous requests and demands to explain my views.

I speak only for myself and not the public affairs committee, though my views are in line with the report of this committee which was unanimously adopted.

I oppose the posting of the Ten Commandments in public classrooms but not because I do not strongly approve this great moral code nor because I do not favor every fair and legal way to improve the moral conditions in public schools. I oppose this because of my strong convictions concerning separation of church and state. I simply don't believe public schools provided partly by taxes collected by law from atheists and other non-Christians as well as Christians should be used to promote the Christian religion. I believe this responsibility was given by God to churches and to homes.

I realize this project is not financed by state funds except those involved in the services of the state Department of Education in this project. The sponsors of House Bill 156 were smart enough to know this could not be done constitutionally, but when this Scripture passage goes on classroom walls it surely puts the state in the role of sponsoring religion.

I am aware of the claim that America was founded on biblical principles including the Ten Commandments and therefore such use of Scripture in public schoolrooms is appropriate. It is true that Christian principles and the Bible inspired many of our founding fathers and the Judeo-Christian ethic was written into many civil documents. I am glad for this and I have profited by it.

However, the same founding fathers demanded that the state stay out of promoting or hindering religion and meant to guarantee this by adding the First Amendment to the constitution. This amendment has consistently been interpreted by the courts as prohibiting the sponsorship of religion by the state. On this basis prayer and Bible reading in public schools were declared unconstitutional.

For this reason House Bill 156 is now in a court suit to determine its constitutionality. It is true that the first court order which prohibited the state Department of Education from implementing this legislation did not prohibit efforts to raise funds for this project. But it seems very questionable to conduct a fund-raising campaign to buy Ten Commandment plaques until they are declared legal by the courts. Should this law be declared unconstitutional and these plaques have to come down and end up gathering dust on closet shelves, what will fund-raising enthusiasts say to sincere people who were led to sacrifice in order to buy these plaques? The nation and Kentucky have survived so far without the Ten Commandments on schoolroom walls. They probably would survive until this litigation is settled.

Apart from the church-state separation principle, a sense of fair play makes this project highly questionable. Fair-minded Christians who post their Scripture passage on public schoolroom walls would be morally bound to defend the right of all other religious groups to post their sacred writings on the same walls. This would include the humanist creed of atheists which declares there is no God and Moslems who claim the true God is Allah. Public classrooms in Kentucky do not have many children of non-Christian religions, but there are some and they have their rights. Baptists of all people have stood for equal treatment of all religious persuasions. Think of the absurdity of having a half-dozen different religious writings, some contradicting each other, on classroom walls.

Baptists fled England and the continent in the 17th century because one religion was favored over others by the state, and they came to America determined to found a nation where no religion was sponsored by civil government. When the Massachusetts Bay Colony government gave preferential treatment to Congregationalism, Baptists fled to Rhode Island and ultimately to Virginia and the Carolinas. When Virginia made the Episcopal church the state religion, Baptists objected and moved to Kentucky. Now some Baptists in Kentucky want to use state-financed schools to sponsor religion in the form of the Ten Commandments. How quickly we forget when we become the majority!

Those who want to display the Ten Commandments and otherwise bring religion into schoolrooms should start and pay for church schools for that purpose. Roman Catholics have been doing this historically and more and more Baptist churches are now doing the same. This is their right and they are to be admired for following their convictions. But having deserted the public schools for their own schools, their efforts to inject religion into public schools paid for by non-Christians as well as Christians seems a little out of place.

No matter how much we want Christian principles in American life, we must remember Christianity is not the official religion of America. Through American history there have been those who have attempted to marry state and church, but discerning Christian statesmen including outstanding Baptists have prevented it. They did not want America to become another Italy or a Spain or go the way of Iran where the head of the dominant religion has taken over the government and has his opponents shot.

I doubt if the reasons given above for my convictions have changed many minds. I only ask for the same right to my convictions as I grant to those who disagree with me.

A claim is being made that Kentucky Baptist denominational workers are to support and work on behalf of this project because it was officially approved by the convention last November. Executive Secretary Frank Owen has said in his weekly columns in *Western Recorder* that contributions sent to the convention for this purpose will be used accordingly so far as the law allows. However, the convention action was not understood to make this a denominational project.

The best understanding of Baptist polity is that no convention actions bind the conscience of every member. Convention action represents the views of the majority of those messengers present. With Baptists the majority prevails but the convictions of the minority are recognized and respected.

As for the public affairs committee, it has received no assignment from the convention except to "keep the Kentucky Baptist

Convention advised on all matters of particular interest to Baptists taking place at the state, national and international levels with particular reference to the separation of church and state." The committee regards its action February 1 as faithfulness to this assignment.

Space in this publication is offered those who want to respond to the statement of the public affairs committee and to the above editorial. (February 21, 1979)

DALEY OBSERVATIONS ON
KENTUCKY BAPTISTS

A MOUNTAIN MIRACLE

I STOOD ON A HIGH HILL OVERLOOKING THE valley where Goose Creek and Red Bird Creek come together to form the South Fork of the Kentucky River. Below me were the fertile acres of the creek bottoms and around me was the quiet little village of Oneida. I was on the campus of Oneida Baptist Institute for the baccalaureate service of the 50th year of this unique school. The fertile acres below me belonged to the school and in the distance a group of school boys was clearing a hedgerow. Corn planting time was at hand, and farming is important to Oneida.

When Oneida Institute, a high school for boarding and day students, began 50 years ago through the efforts of James Anderson Burns, it provided the only educational opportunity for many mountain boys and girls isolated by distances and mountainous terrain. Boys and girls walked miles to the school to spend the week and miles back home over mountains and up creeks. Most of these young people possessed only keen minds and intense desire to become enlightened and find their places in this world. From the school have gone prominent men and women to many places of the world. President Sparks is proud of the fact that Oneida graduates of recent years are now enrolled in a score or more colleges and universities.

Now that roads, school buses and free public schools have made something of a new world for the mountains, Oneida still fills a unique place. This year's class, just as all the classes through the years, has students whose stories sound more like fiction than fact. President D. Chester Sparks, standing with me as the procession began into the Oneida Baptist Church, told me the highlights of several of the graduates. Many parents were present, coming varying distances. The father of one graduate is a Mennonite missionary who spoke glowingly of Oneida's contribution to several of his children who have attended the school. Not present were the parents of two fine, clean-cut Iranian boys in the class.

One especially attractive girl was pointed out to me by President Sparks. Coming from a very large family with severely limited means, her training at Oneida had been sponsored by Miss Clara McCartt, secretary to Dr. Duke K. McCall, Southern Seminary president. The young lady has a burning ambition to be a nurse. She plans to enter training in the Kentucky Baptist Hospital and will continue to have the counsel and help of Miss McCartt.

The school choir provided a beautiful rendition following the message just as had a sextet earlier in the service. The choir was immaculately robed. It was the first time they had worn the robes which had been given to Oneida by a Baptist church in Brooklyn, N.Y. The latest effort of the music department is the formation of a band. Instruments are needed, and since the students will not be able to provide their own, some Kentucky Baptists and friends of the school will want to contribute an instrument. The Sparkses will be proud to receive any instrument in working condition.

The first graduates of Oneida were honored at commencement exercises this year. A mountain cabin has been erected on the edge of the campus as a memorial to James Anderson Burns. Known as "Burns of the Mountains," this unusual character turned from a fightin', feudin' timber floater to a Baptist preacher and teacher. He gave his life, talent and wealth to found this school which others said would never succeed. But succeed it did. President Sparks regretted that a recent *Courier-Journal* article featuring the school called it "interdenominational." For while students of many faiths enroll, Oneida is truly a Baptist school. Its main source of income is from Kentucky Baptists. President Sparks is a widely known Baptist preacher and his faculty is composed of dedicated Baptist teachers.

James Anderson Burns is said to have died possessing only his clothes, a Bible and a radio, but thousands of boys and girls have received inestimable riches through the school he founded. To many, Oneida is nothing less than a mountain miracle. (May 8, 1958)

EARLY DAYS OF THE KENTUCKY BAPTIST CONVENTION

WHEN HUNDREDS OF KENTUCKY BAPTISTS gather at Harlan next week for the 120th session of the General Association, it will be a far cry from the first time the Baptists of Kentucky met in an effort to cooperate in missionary endeavor. This was way back in 1831 when after two successful attempts, Dr. S.M. Noel, pastor at Frankfort, and Rev. John S. Wilson of Todd County succeeded in getting a few Baptists together to consider the possibility of a state organization for Baptists. The result was the formation of the Kentucky Baptist

Convention in 1832 at Bardstown. The convention was held in the Presbyterian meeting house, only 34 messengers were listed, $190.67 was the total finances but "many were awakened, and we trust not a few renewed. Six were received and baptized on the Lord's Day."

In spite of the devoted efforts of several early Baptist leaders like Noel and Wilson and Dr. J.M. Pendleton, who rode on horseback from Hopkinsville to New Castle for a later meeting, the Kentucky Baptist Convention was destined to be of short life and to be even shorter on popular approval and cooperation. When it ceased to exist in 1837, the enemies of missions and cooperation rejoiced, but it had succeeded in preparing the way for the permanent state organization which started in 1837 and continues with God's blessings to this good hour.

The beginnings of Kentucky Baptists in organized work were not marked with any great prospects. When the General Association was brought into existence at the Baptist meeting house in Louisville (later to be First Baptist and now Walnut Street), there was only one Baptist congregation of 380 members for the 25,000 Louisville population. As late as 1867 there were only three Louisville Baptist churches with 1,200 members for a population of 140,000 and by 1878 there were only 35 full-time Baptist churches in Kentucky. More than 100 churches and missions reported this year in the Louisville area alone give us reason to praise the Lord for undreamed of blessings and advance.

Interesting incidents connected with meetings of the General Association would fill a book. For instance, it might be surprising to know that from the beginning we have had an executive secretary heading up the work in the whole state. In early days he was known as the general agent and his duties were much the same as today except that one of his main responsibilities was to urge churches to pay their pastors a living wage. Then just as now he gave the annual financial report including his own expenses. A sample is the report of General Agent W.C. Buck in 1838 for the month of June, which included horse shoeing 75¢, ferriage 12¢, toll gate fare 25¢, and keeping horse in Louisville for four nights $2. Not many of us could get to Harlan on that.

There were three classes of members of the General Association in 1853; first, elected messengers from local churches and associations; second, life members, composed of those who paid $30 into the treasury of the body; and third, annual members who paid one dollar. The record shows 27 messengers from churches and associations, 20 annual members and 62 life members, of whom eight were women. I doubt if many Kentucky Baptists today know that in 1853 life membership in the General Association could be bought by individuals for $30 and that women were counted.

Twice, in 1857 and in 1870, the General Association and the Southern Baptist Convention met in Louisville and the sessions were so scheduled that messengers could take advantage of both meetings. Almost unbelievable is the account that both the Southern Convention and General Association met simultaneously in Russellville, Ky., in the year 1866 with one group using the morning and the other the afternoon for sessions.

And then there are many incidents connected with the General Association meetings not found in the minutes, such as the 1939 session in Harrodsburg when, during the time of the meeting a large sum of money mysteriously disappeared from a local bank, which, I am told, has never been accounted for though bank officials are still looking for prosperous-appearing Baptist preachers.

A marvelous thing to remember is that whether it is a score of messengers in 1837 arriving at the association by way of one horse power each or a thousand messengers coming in 1957 by way of 220 horse power horseless carriages, we are both convening to carry out the words of our Master who said to the first association of disciples, "Go ye therefore, and teach all nations, baptizing them in the name of the Father, and of the Son, and of the Holy Ghost." (November 7, 1957)

REVIVAL AND SPRING IN JELLICO

A SPIRITUAL REVIVAL AT THE FIRST BAPTIST
Church in Jellico, Tenn., and nature's revival of spring
beauty in the surrounding Appalachian landscape arrived the
same week. The abundant showers and warm sunshine of early
April gave birth to mountain springtime over night. The tender,
pale, green leaves seemed to double in size every day and what
was but a hint of pink yesterday is a bright red-bud cloud against
a green hillside today. Nowhere in the world could the celebration of the Resurrection of God's Son be timed more perfectly
with the resurrection of God's world.

And hardly anywhere in the world can be found a church
with a more significant past and present. Though now associated
with the Tennessee Baptist Convention, Jellico's First Baptist
Church began and continued most of its years as a significant
part of Kentucky's fellowship. Among its chartered members in
1884 were the names of Smith, Siler and Mahan which are still
familiar Kentucky Baptist names, especially in the Williamsburg
area. For many years the Kentucky Baptist Mission Board paid
part of the pastor's salary of this church which was begun by
devout people of God to offset the worldliness that invaded the
area with the coming of the lumber and coal boom of eastern
Tennessee and Kentucky.

The first church house was a $700 one-room structure. The
present building dates from 1913 and is of exquisite beauty and
great usefulness. The Jellico church has had an unusual number
of outstanding pastors and this doubtlessly accounts for the high
spiritual level of past and present congregations. Another testimony to the caliber of the church is the unusual love that has
existed through the years between the people and the pastors.

One of the really significant dates and events of Kentucky
Baptists and Southern Baptist history is related to Jellico's First

Baptist Church. It was at the 1915 General Association meeting of Kentucky Baptists in Jellico that the Cooperative Program idea was born. Called the Budget System when it was adopted at the meeting, it was used by Kentucky Baptists from 1915 on and later adopted by the Southern Baptist Convention as the Cooperative Program.

Western Recorder editor J.W. Porter, editorializing on this 1915 General Association meeting in the November 20, 1915, issue, used these significant words: "The most important act of the body was the adoption of the Budget System. This plan will save the needless multiplication of unnecessary collection agencies, and tend to develop proportionate and uniform giving." How prophetic were his words!

The present Jellico congregation lives up to the illustrious past. The love between the congregation and Pastor Dick Allison and his wife, Jane, is something wonderful to behold. Dick and Jane are both Kentuckians. We were first associated at Georgetown College in the early 1950s and later, while Dick finished Southern Seminary and was pastor of Barren Run Church near Hodgenville, Jane was secretary for the *Western Recorder* editor.

The current records of the Jellico congregation reflect noble efforts in the face of difficult circumstances. The lumber has long been gone and the coal which is now mechanically mined requires few workers. The population of Jellico is several hundred less than when the General Association was held in 1915, and a high percentage of the area's population is on welfare. Still the income of the church is higher than ever and most phases of church life have never been so strong.

On his General Association visit to Jellico in 1915, *Western Recorder* Editor Porter said, "The hospitality of the Jellico saints was all that could be asked, and possibly greater than ever before accorded the messengers and visitors." This *Western Recorder* editor found the same in Jellico in 1965. (April 22, 1965)

PIANIST GONE, SINGING CONTINUES

IN SPITE OF THE RAIN WHICH BEAT LOUDLY ON the tin roof of the one-room building, we were singing "At the Cross" and "Blessed Assurance." An added difficulty in singing was the absence of any musical accompaniment, though a piano stood in one corner of the large room. Until several months ago a beautiful, consecrated high school girl had played the piano each Sunday afternoon, but now she was gone and there was nobody to play. Her body lay buried on a mountainside several miles away, her spirit lingered in many hearts though she had joined the celestial choir of glory. She was one of the 26 Prestonsburg high school boys and girls plunged into a watery grave in the tragic school bus accident this spring.

I was in Prestonsburg to supply for Pastor Ira McMillen Jr., who has been sent by the Irene Cole Memorial Baptist Church on a world tour. Deacon Terry was the pastor of the week and invited me to go with him in the afternoon to Benedict Chapel, a mission named for the beloved former pastor, L.W. Benedict. Benedict Chapel is one of two missions of which Deacon Terry is superintendent.

We exchanged a car for a pickup truck and left town in the rain. As it continued to pour I felt a little embarrassed for the deacon, because I knew he wanted me to see the mission at its best and I was afraid no one would brave the rain, even if we managed to reach the mission on the mountain road. We turned off Highway 23, where Cow Creek empties into Levisa Fork and where stands the home and store of the James Gobels. A few yards up Cow Creek on the mountainside above the road I could see through the rain artificial flowers covering three real graves. In them were the three Gobel children—all the children of the Gobels. They had perished in the tragedy.

Soon we turned off Cow Creek and started up Slick Rock. With some difficulty we reached Benedict Chapel and to my surprise children were waiting in the rain. By the time Deacon Terry made another trip for another load of people, others had come in from nearby houses, and the service started with 65 men, women, boys and girls. There were 13 Intermediates, most of whom had been together all day with their teacher. They had brought picnic lunch and visited the graves of their four former classmates who had perished in the wreck.

After Sunday School I was invited to preach, and it was an unforgettable experience. One of my most attentive listeners was Uncle John Darby, whose house we had passed back down the hollow. He is 66 years old and has 10 grown children. Of his two other children not living, one was a high school senior lost in the accident. Two of his grandchildren were also victims. Uncle John through many years had rejected all invitations to profess faith in Christ, though many of his children were devoted Christians. The daughter who perished had written about a year earlier to a preacher giving a beautiful testimony of her love for the Lord. Feeling the hand of the Lord, Uncle John accepted Christ publicly recently, as have 16 others since the accident.

After the service we stopped by to see Aunt Vate Herald. At 83 she is still bright and radiant, and is known as one who has never missed an opportunity to witness to others. Aunt Vate spent most of her life as a member of another faith but a year or so ago was baptized into a Baptist church because, as she says, of what she discovered in her Bible study. Around one like Aunt Vate there is never a doubt of how the visit is to be ended, nor is there any doubt but that God is near when prayer is offered together.

On the way back to town we stopped where the school bus plunged into Levisa Fork. The highway shoulder was worn smooth from the thousands who had stopped to see the place. Across the river were the marks on the bank where the battered bus had been dragged out. The banks below were strewn with the willows pulled out of the river's edge in search of bodies. Even deeper than the shock of thinking of the lost lives of bright-eyed boys and girls was the thought of how many of their souls were also lost and how much of their blood will be required of my hands as a Kentucky Baptist.

You have to see the life of the Irene Cole Baptist Church to believe it. In the bulletin last Sunday were 12 missions listed, some in the morning, some in the afternoon. Every deacon except one who is giving his time as a lay preacher is in charge of at least one mission. Some miss Sunday School to go to a mission. The editor of the local paper excused himself from the morning worship to go work in a mission. In all, about 50 people are engaged every Sunday in these 12 missions where combined attendance often exceeds 400. I have a new understanding of the description of the New Testament church, "And they went forth, and preached everywhere, the Lord working with them." (June 12, 1958)

BOONE LODGE IS A MEMORABLE EXPERIENCE

IT IS WEDNESDAY AFTERNOON, DECEMBER 2, THE day before the dedication of Boone Lodge at Cedarmore Baptist Assembly. Looking out the window of Room 204 of the lodge, one could wonder if he is in Switzerland, the Appalachians, the Rockies or some other spot of unsurpassing beauty. The steep hills of Shelby County rival any of these far away places for sheer beauty.

Underneath the lodge window meanders picturesque Dragon Lake, now half frozen over. On the sharply rising hill beyond the lake persistently green cedars speak of life as they stand among the naked sleeping maples, sweetgums and sycamores.

Rooming with Hodgenville Pastor Jim Coker, we decided on a little trek along the lake for some exercise and fresh air following the conclusion of the preview study of Deuteronomy.

Naturally, I felt better walking with a gun, especially since a flock of large black ducks breaking their trip from the north to warmer climes had been seen circling the lake. Preacher-like we were engaged in lively conversation and peanut eating as we walked along the trail beside the lake. Suddenly a flock of large ducks flushed from a nearby spot on the lake. Without our noisy approach we surely could have gotten close enough to have had roast duck. Our experience ruined our sermons on busy and noisy tongues.

Boone Lodge is a dream come true. Those familiar with Cedarmore as it has appeared through the years are simply over-whelmed when they first visit the new lodge. It is not luxurious, but is as practical, beautiful and comfortable as any Baptist could desire. It offers to Kentucky Baptists the most ideal facilities for the much needed periodic renewal of body and soul.

An indispensable part of the inviting hospitality of Boone Lodge is the service of Mr. and Mrs. Marvin Byrdwell. The Byrdwells and Cedarmore go together like bread and butter — one would not be worth much without the other. The faithful and effi-cient ministry of the Byrdwells at Cedarmore through the years of woefully inadequate facilities certainly entitles them to the oppor-tunity now to direct the activities at the improved facilities.

Capable staff members, from the friendly ladies at the desk to those keeping the grounds immaculately and those preparing and serving the delicious meals, make Cedarmore and Boone Lodge a memorable experience.

It was fitting that Dr. W.C. Boone and Dr. Elroy Lamb be invited back for the dedication of the lodge. Dr. Boone was the beloved executive secretary of Kentucky Baptists through the years of early Cedarmore development, and Dr. Lamb was chairman of the Cedarmore committee when the lodge was first recommended several years ago.

But if Dr. Boone was the David who dreamed and prepared for the construction of the lodge, Dr. Harold Sanders is the

Solomon who brought realization to the dream. And his imagination and vision produced something far beyond the expectations of most Kentucky Baptists.

It now remains for the Baptists of Kentucky to glorify God through the use of Boone Lodge. We have glorious facilities, we must now have activities befitting the facilities. We're off to a good start. The January Bible Study preview led by Dr. Donald Ackland, the author of this year's Bible study manual, brought pastors this week from all over the state to return prepared to lead their congregations in a meaningful Bible study in January.

With the conclusion of these lines, it's time to hit the hay. The soft rain falling from the roof of the lodge is like magic from heaven. When my eyes close I'll still see the majestic ducks gliding along the bosom of Dragon Lake and the thousands of Kentucky Baptists who will find their inspiration at Cedarmore in the coming years. If the Lord had made the earth any better, who would want to go to heaven? (December 10, 1964)

SHE HATH DONE WHAT SHE COULD

ONCE UPON A TIME THE GOOD OLE SUMMERTIME was the most inspiring time in a Baptist church. The climax of every year was the annual protracted meeting when crowds overflowed the church into the church yard. The schedules of the members were arranged to fit the meeting. The hens were set in time for the little chicks to be frying size by revival time. Beans, corn, tomatoes and watermelons were planted to be ready for the preachers and other company during the meeting.

Generally the meeting was the same time each year so relatives and friends living away from home could plan their annual visit with home folks during revival time. The week or weeks of the revival had to fall between laying-by time and time to harvest the crop. (For the younger generation laying-by is that time when the crop is ploughed the last time and the farmer takes it easy waiting for harvest time.)

That's the way it used to be with Baptists in the summertime. Not so now. Instead of being the most inspiring time, summer in most Baptist churches now is anything but inspiring. Revivals have long since been moved to the fall and spring. In the summertime church attendance lags and offerings sag as church members by the droves try to get away from it all, including their churches. Travel, boating, camping and other vacation activities leave many empty pews in Baptist churches during the summer months.

Those of us who do denominational work and visit many churches are accustomed to the explanations and apologies offered for the summer slump. They are about the same wherever one goes. The hope is to hold things together somehow until September comes when things return to normalcy.

It would be easy to become discouraged if we looked only at the statistics of Baptist churches today in the summertime. On the other hand when we look beyond statistics, there are reasons to be encouraged. When things are at their worst, some of God's servants are at their best. And all the saints are not dead and gone. We have in our churches today some of the most dedicated Christians who ever lived. There are many examples of sacrificial service that set the soul to singing.

One such example of loving service almost overwhelmed me on a recent Sunday when I was supply preacher for the day. The little church was more than 100 miles from Louisville on the edge of Appalachia. The pastor and his family were on a much deserved vacation. This meant not only the worship leader was absent but the pastor's wife who played the organ. But even this was still not so bad since a gifted pianist was left to carry on the music.

But, alas, the pianist was called out of town due to the illness of her father. This meant neither musicians nor the pastor were present to lead the service. The pastor's place was not too difficult a problem. A young layman who was trained at Georgetown College was able and willing to lead the service.

But what about someone to play the piano? The one other person who had ever played for worship services was a dear woman who was now seriously afflicted with arthritis. Her fingers had been so affected that she could not close her hand. Surgery on her hands had helped a little and made it possible for her to move her fingers slightly.

With her stiff hand and twisted fingers she could not reach all the notes, but there she was trying to play for the song service. Her playing was seriously hampered and many notes were missed. By human standards she was a failure, but by God's standards she surely was given an A plus.

She made no apology and none was in order. It was the kind of music to set angels to singing. Through the human discord there seemed to be a divine voice saying, "She hath done what she could; ... Wheresoever this gospel shall be preached throughout the whole world, this also that she hath done shall be spoken of for a memorial of her" (Mark 13: 8-9).

Her loving act was a more effective sermon than could ever come from a visiting preacher. Indeed, it was a sermon the visiting preacher needed. (July 10, 1969)

ASSOCIATION TIME

IT'S ASSOCIATION TIME! MODERATOR GAMMON'S gavel called Simpson Association to order at Middleton on Wednesday of this week and other gavels will be falling from now to October 23 when Graves County convenes at Pilot Oak. From Enterprise and the Big Sandy on the Virginia-West Virginia border all the way to West Kentucky Association on the Mississippi looking into Missouri, and from the North Bend up Cincinnati way all the way down to Jellico, Tenn., Kentucky

Baptists will be gathering to rejoice in the Lord's blessings during the past year and to resolve nobler endeavor for him another year. Some of the meetings will be in city churches with hotel-like eating facilities, but by far most of them will be in church houses where the yard is the dining room, leafy maple trees shelter and wagon beds the tables.

There'll be baskets of fried chicken, platters of old ham, dozens of dressed eggs, sandwiches, pickles, stacked cakes, layer cakes, jam cakes, pies of every imaginable kind, iced tea and coffee, carrels of cold water, everything else wonderful Baptist women can think of, and flies. There'll be deacons, preachers, boys and girls, women and babies, young people and state workers. Standing around after dinner the deacons will talk about the preachers, the preachers will talk about the deacons, and both of them will remark about how fat and prosperous the state workers all look. Boys and girls from different churches will pair off to sit in automobiles for a little fellowship of kindred spirits, some of the men will have a smoke and few will even take a chew of long green, and the resolutions committee will meet under a tree on the other side of the church.

Inside some preacher will edify the brethren with a doctrinal sermon, a state worker given five minutes will take 15, oratory and resolutions on the liquor problem will follow the report on civic righteousness, and a good-natured but serious argument will develop on some minor point during the period for miscellaneous business. In some places the ladies will not get up to give the WMU report because of Paul's words, but they will all stand up to prepare lunch before the annual sermon starts. Somebody will ask why it took so long last year to get the associational minutes and somebody else will want to know why you don't still address Dr. W.C. Boone at 127 E. Broadway.

This is the association, next to the annual revival, the most enjoyable church event of the year to many Baptists. It's been going on a long time. The first association could have been when

Jerusalem and Antioch churches met around A.D. 50 to discuss a common problem and settle an important issue. There was wholesome debate on that occasion which worked out for the glory of God and so has it been since then. Five General Baptist churches cooperated in associational activity in England as early as 1624 and in America the Philadelphia Association was formed in 1707 for fellowship, inspiration and evangelism. Sixteen messengers from six Kentucky churches met at Clear Creek, in Woodford County, on Friday, September 30, 1785, and on the next day, October 1, constituted Elkhorn Association, the first in Kentucky. Today, 172 years later, in Kentucky there are 81 associations embracing 2,254 churches and 589,807 Baptists.

The district association is not only a delightful event but in some respects the most important event for Baptists in their effort to carry out the Great Commission. This is where churches which are completely independent voluntarily cooperate to foster district, state and world enterprises. It would be difficult to conceive of God's mighty movement through the ages among Baptists apart from this principle of association and, for this reason, it is not much to consider that it was inspired and nurtured by the head of the church. Churches which resist this kind of cooperation are rejecting a part of Baptist faith and practice validated by divine blessings throughout history. The job is too big and the time too short for a single church to try to get the good news to every creature. While every church should work as if it all depended upon one church, every church should cooperate with all other true churches as if it required every church. See you at the association! (July 25, 1957)

THE BICENTENNIAL CELEBRATION IN HARRODSBURG

NO GATHERING COULD HAVE BEEN MORE typically "Baptist." It was one of those "Amazing Grace" and "On Jordan's Stormy Banks I Stand" kind of meetings. We had old-time religion and even old-time sweating thanks to July weather and a malfunctioning air conditioning system.

The bicentennial celebration of Kentucky Baptist preaching on April 19 was billed as a major Baptist event in Kentucky. It lived up to its billing and even surpassed highest expectations.

Baptists from all areas of Kentucky descended upon Harrodsburg to celebrate, and celebrate we did. From the east, the west, the north and the south they came. They overflowed the spacious Harrodsburg sanctuary. They worshipped, they prayed, they amened and they sang "We're Marching to Zion" while parading down Harrodsburg streets.

There was something deeply moving about the experience. We rejoiced in recalling a noble heritage, exulted in the wonder of being redeemed and sincerely longed to perpetuate our noble heritage of gospel preaching.

The preaching was great as expected but the music surpassed every dream. We planned it as a day of preaching with music; it turned out to be a day of singing with preaching. There is no account of the gospel music in that first outdoor Baptist service in 1776 but the music of the bicentennial celebration will live as long as the preaching.

Probably the greatest and longest-lasting impression of the day will be the part of black Baptists in the celebration. Their response and participation are a tribute to their leaders and to the cordial relationship between black and white Baptists in Kentucky. The joint black-white planning committee for the occasion did a magnificent job. Behind this pleasing experience of interracial worship and fellowship can be seen the effective work of Bill Rogers, our Kentucky Baptist director of interracial ministries.

Whatever the blacks came to receive, they gave more than they took away. Any doubt about the high quality of the preaching and singing of black Baptists was removed for everyone in the Harrodsburg celebration. In fact, it is really unfair to compare the music and praise of blacks and whites. Whether it is a native gift or a result of long suffering and yearning, there is a dimension of black singing unknown to whites. If whites had done as much with their abundance of resources as blacks have with their meager resources, the Kingdom might already have come in.

Certainly each milestone celebration of Baptist preaching in Kentucky has had its special characteristics. For the 200th anniversary the one quality which was not present in the others was major participation of black Baptists. For this we rejoice because, as one speaker said, such a joint celebration would not have been possible 20 years ago.

It has taken us 200 years to learn to practice some of the truths we preached from the beginning. We have come a long way and still have a long way to go. But we marked a significant milestone in Harrodsburg in 1976 and we're marching on.

The hospitality of Harrodsburg and Mercer County Baptists added to the joy of the occasion. In fact this day of celebration brought out the best of all of us. It even produced a poem from Executive Secretary Frank Owen who used it to climax one of the best addresses he has ever made in his leadership ministry with Kentucky Baptists.

Yes, we put it all together in Harrodsburg. (April 29, 1976)

WITH GOD'S SERVANTS IN THE MOUNTAINS

KENTUCKY BAPTISTS HAVE A WIDE VARIETY OF conferences, assemblies and camps to choose from each summer. Among the most unique and rewarding of these summer conferences is the Mountain Missions Conference sponsored by the Kentucky Baptist missions department and held on the campus of Oneida Baptist Institute. This editor was one of the participants in this year's conference who will cherish its memories and blessings a long time.

This was the second year for this gathering of those who minister in the challenging mountains of Eastern Kentucky. In earlier years it was for pastors only but now it is a family affair. And so the ring of children's laughter and the cheery chatter of pastors' wives are heard along with the serious and light conversations of preachers.

The affair is a delightful blend of worship, study, rest and fellowship. The accent is on informality with coats and ties almost never seen. Everyone is in classes and conferences during the morning and separate worship services for adults and youth are the order for the early evening. The rest of the time is free for all the happy activities preachers and their family members enjoy. For some who attend it is the only real vacation of the year.

The setting on the Oneida campus seems an indispensable part of the experience. Chairs are set up under the stately trees atop the hill on which the school stands. Couples who have this one opportunity each year to visit each other engage in happy conversation. Preachers gather in small or large groups to swap experiences, to settle theological issues or just to whittle while engaging in light talk. Some parents swim, play tennis and ping-pong or otherwise frolic with their children. And it is not unusual to see a preacher and his wife holding hands while strolling across the campus. Laughter rings across the campus late into the night and spontaneous singing of children and adults occasionally breaks out and fills the night air.

Architects for this annual affair are Bob Jones, director of the Kentucky Baptist mountain missions program, and A.B. Colvin, Kentucky Baptist missions secretary. To watch these two men work together and to see the relationship which exists between them and these preachers in the mountains is to understand the spirit and success of the conference.

The week provided many blessings for this participant but two stand to have the most permanent effects. One was the experience of rooming with James Rose who was one of these mountain pastors before he felt led by the Lord to extend his ministry to Southern Baptists through the Southern Baptist Sunday School Board. His compassion and concern are as big as the mountains he still loves and they rub off on all those around him.

The other special blessing came at the end of the final Bible study hour when a spontaneous confession and testimony service seemed to bring heaven down to fill our souls. Such high moments are not experienced often enough by this writer but they are worth waiting for and remembering. (August 1, 1970)

A BEDTIME STORY

ONCE UPON A TIME THERE WAS A GROUP OF people called Southern Baptists. They grew from a small number to a mighty host of people in a shorter time than most other religious groups had ever grown.

These people called Baptists believed strongly in individualism and put great stress on personal freedom. They would have nothing to do with bishops and other ecclesiastical authorities. They thought that every person should read the Bible for himself and with the help of the Holy Spirit arrive at his own convictions. They considered every church completely in control of its own affairs.

These Baptists had many things in common including the same convictions on the great doctrines found in the Bible, but possessed great varieties of beliefs on many other details of doctrine and polity.

At first most of the Baptist churches because of their individualism and independence went their own way and had little to do with other Baptist churches. Some even believed that it was wrong to join with other Baptist churches in trying to send missionaries or do other things one church could not do by itself. Sometimes Baptists disagreed with some of the professors but still loved them; some criticized the teachers but still supported the seminaries. These seminaries continued to prosper, grew in number and attracted many of the brightest young people from Baptist churches.

But before long they learned to love one another and work together willingly. They did this first in order to support missionaries and have schools in which to train missionaries and preachers. This worked so fine that they joined together to build many great institutions and agencies for carrying out the Great Commission. This plan was so successful that only few Baptists and Baptist churches did not join in gladly.

Because Baptists believe so strongly in the Bible, they considered it important to have preachers who could preach and teach the great truths of the Bible. For this purpose they built Baptist schools and seminaries to train their preachers. To these schools and seminaries went thousands of young men and women to prepare for what the Lord called them to do.

In the early days of the Baptist seminaries, there was a good spirit though there was some criticism.

By and by things changed. Some of the bright seminary students became teachers in the seminaries. They went away to non-Baptist schools for advanced training and heard new and interesting viewpoints and interpretations of the Bible. Some of these things they did not believe; others seemed to them to be nearer right than what they had heard from childhood. They were honest enough to say so and this got them into trouble.

Occasionally, a seminary teacher seemed to be immature and carried away with most any new viewpoint. He accepted as truth what was only theory and passed it on to students. Sometimes he was even cynical about some beliefs most Baptists held very precious through the years. Most of the seminary teachers, however, diligently and honestly searched for truth and courageously talked about what they found.

In turn there arose a good many critics of the seminaries and these teachers. Some of these critics were either insincere, sincere but misinformed, conscious or unconscious attention seekers, or just plain critics of anything and anybody but theirs and themselves.

Other critics were responsible and sincere. They had justified concern for doctrinal purity and sound biblical scholarship in Baptist seminaries. They feared the theological liberalism and modernism which had overtaken other denominations.

One of the sad things about all this was that fellow Baptists seemed to lose respect and love for each other. One was not willing to tolerate another unless the other agreed completely with him. Instead of sitting down with the seminary professor to discuss the matter, the critic assumed he understood completely the teacher's position and labeled it heresy.

Sadder still, the critics apparently assumed that the presidents and duly elected trustees could not be trusted to save Baptist seminaries from false teaching, and so sent off tirades to all the state papers. The seminary presidents and trustees then had to appeal to the editors not to run the criticism lest it do irreparable damage to the seminary and Baptist work in general. A sad state of affairs!

And so what was the most vigorous and dynamic people of God in America became dangerously close to damaging divisiveness and prospective rupture. Only mutual responsibility for self-correction, love and trust toward each other, and common commitment to God's leadership could save this mighty people. Otherwise a bed-time story would end up a death bed account. (November 30, 1961)

THE COOPERATIVE PROGRAM IS GOOD
BUT IS NOT GOD

IN 1968 THE TOTAL REPORTED RECEIPTS OF Southern Baptist churches, agencies and institutions was about $795 million. This means the Southern Baptist enterprise all the way from the local church to the last mission point costs more than $2 million every day of the year. All this comes from voluntary giving and most of it is given through the Cooperative Program.

The requirement of $2 million a day for the worldwide Southern Baptist enterprise dramatically demonstrates the importance of the Cooperative Program and its well-being. This is why any threat to the Cooperative Program causes sleepless nights and reactivated ulcers for denominational leaders.

An illustration is the recent controversial morality conference sponsored by the Southern Baptist Christian Life Commission. When a number of churches and pastors objected to this conference and some of its participants and several churches even voted to withhold Cooperative Program gifts to the denomination, serious concern and opposition to the conference were expressed by several state executives secretaries. (Kentucky Baptist Executive Secretary Harold Sanders was not one of these.) On the grounds that the conference program would hurt the Cooperative Program, at least one state Baptist editor opposed this project as planned.

While such concern is understandable, is not such a philosophy bordering dangerously on compromising expediency? The Cooperative Program and its health are important and are worth more than one morality seminar, but making a judgment based on financial welfare is bordering on, if it is not actual, idolatry.

Such a reverence for the Cooperative Program tends to put a plan of giving above God and this is idolatry. It leads to a tragic kind of reasoning which makes us ask of any thing, not is it right but is it good for the program. One step further leads us to the conclusion if it encourages financial giving it's good, if it discourages financial giving it's bad. And this was the attitude of the masters of the soothsaying damsel of Philippi when she was healed of the spirit of divination. "And when her masters saw that the hope of their gains was gone, they caught Paul and Silas, ... and brought them to the magistrates."

This is a built-in problem with any form of voluntary giving or spending. The quickest and most effective way to get at the beneficiaries of any type of business is economic boycott. This works in a denomination like it does in a business.

The Southern Baptist Sunday School Board faces this problem every day. The income for the board's vast operations depends upon the purchase of materials by churches and individuals. Some churches which object to the doctrinal positions of some materials and to the board's publishing of Training Union units on sex education or other controversial subjects are threatening to boycott the board. Courage and integrity are required on the part of Executive Secretary James L. Sullivan and the Sunday School Board members not to give in to such economic threats. The same goes for the leadership of every denominational agency and institution.

Such a dilemma may be more of a blessing than first appears. Surely churches and individuals have the right to protest and a boycott of giving or buying literature is a valid form of protest. Denominational leaders should have to answer for all their policies and they should always be sensitive to the thinking of the Baptist masses.

On the other hand denominational leaders must have the courage and integrity to stand on principle and not compromise for expediency's sake. If any denominational leader is not strong enough to risk popularity, position and worldly success for truth and right, it ought to be revealed.

What does all this mean? It means these are times that try the soul of every Baptist whether he is on the giving or receiving end. It means those who give should exercise their right not to give very cautiously. Their decision should be made on the basis of conscience enlightened by God's revelation and not on personal likes and dislikes. It means denominational leaders must remain sensitive and responsive to the views of the Baptist masses but must never compromise principle for expediency. It's better to go out of business than to sell one's soul to stay in. The Cooperative Program is good but it is not God. (April 11, 1970)

DEACONS AND BAPTIST DEMOCRACY

A WIDESPREAD COMPLAINT AMONG BAPTISTS today is that our churches are not democratic. The most frequent criticism is that deacons and other church leaders dominate the church and decide what is to be done before the church members even hear about it.

Many Baptists are asking how much authority do deacons have and whether or not all items of business must come through the deacons to the church. The simple answer is that a Baptist church does as it chooses. It even has the choice of using or not using deacons and assigning to them whatever duties it chooses. A Baptist church, however, is always under obligation to follow the New Testament in all its affairs, including those related to deacons.

What does the New Testament say? The answer here is not simple as we sometimes make it sound. The New Testament describes the actual circumstances of the early churches and how deacons came to be used by these churches in carrying out their Christ-given assignment.

By now conditions and circumstances have changed. For example, what Baptist church today elects deacons to distribute necessities of life to widows on the benevolent rolls as was the case of the first deacons? The value of the New Testament, then, is in the principles found there concerning deacons. But even these principles are not easily found.

It's easier to pattern the church after the world around us than after the New Testament because we spend so much more time looking at the world than we do examining the New Testament. Maybe this has happened to some Baptist churches. We are surrounded by a business world in which established practices are accepted, and it is very easy to baptize these procedures for church use. This is altogether proper when these business procedures are consistent with New Testament principles.

The violation would seem to come when the church becomes a business operation more than a witnessing community of saints. In such a business operation the deacons become a board of directors and the pastor the company president. Like company directors, the deacons are chosen for the number of shares they own in the business and for their ability to manage the venture efficiently and profitably. "In the black" becomes more important than "in the spirit" and boasting of statistics replaces humility of service.

In such a situation the rest of the church members feel left out. They get the impression that only the official recommendations of the deacons are considered worthy of consideration by the congregation. They feel that they are not considered wise enough to be trusted and only those in the know are really qualified to direct policy. To question the official recommendation is to act foolish, if not to become downright undesirable.

This may be overstating the case, for not many churches are dominated by deacons to this extent. And when this is the case, the fault is shared jointly by the other church members and the deacons. But let exaggeration serve as a caution because any church operated mainly as a business organization rather than a fellowship of equals is headed for tragedy.

Should other church committees report to the deacons before bringing recommendations to the church? No, unless they are instructed to do so by the church. The deacons are selected by the church for specific responsibilities. Let the deacons report to the church on the stewardship of these responsibilities.

The church selects other committees for other responsibilities. Why not let these committees report just as the deacons do? There is no good reason for other committees to have their recommendations screened by the deacons. If so, why not give the committees' tasks to the deacons in the first place? Only committees of the deacons and those specifically instructed by the church to do so should have to report to the deacons.

If we believe a Baptist church is a fellowship of equals, we ought to practice it. Until we do, many church members will be unhappy, others will laugh at us for saying we are democratic when we are not, and the Lord will frown upon us for saying we are New Testament churches when we are not. (January 10, 1963)

DENOMINATIONAL ORGANIZATION EXISTS FOR CHURCHES' SAKE

THIS COULD SOUND LIKE A STRANGE IF NOT AN unbecoming confession for a denominational worker but it has been a growing conviction of mine which keeps crying for expression. As one whose ministry is mainly with producing a denominational publication, meeting with committees on all levels of denominational life, promoting and evaluating denominational programs, I have difficulty at times not despairing for the future of Southern Baptists in God's redemptive plan for this world.

On the other hand when I visit local congregations of Baptists in Kentucky and some in other states in worship and fellowship experiences, my spirit often soars and my hope is renewed for the Lord's cause among Southern Baptists.

If I were reading the above words instead of writing them, I would be prone to conclude that the writer is out of pocket and should be ministering through a local church instead of being a denominational worker. As the writer I can only reply I am where I believe the Lord wants me as his servant and this is enough inspiration and joy in spite of a solid conviction that the hope for Southern Baptists really is in the local churches.

It is quite natural that a denominational worker whose time is mostly consumed with programs, statistics, budget and denominational problems cannot always feel the thrill that is a pastor's experience with day-by-day personal problems, joys and sorrows. This is not to say a pastor doesn't have to fight to keep from becoming consumed with trivia, promotion and everything else but people.

Whatever has been said above does not mean to imply denominational organization and denominational workers are not vital in the life of Southern Baptists. Indeed, without our denominational structure what Baptist local churches could do in the way of a worldwide missionary evangelistic ministry would be seriously limited. Independent Baptist churches tend to wax and wane in their zeal and ministry beyond the local community while Southern Baptists plod on with an ever-expanding outreach to the whole world.

The redeeming side of denominational work is the privilege of denominational workers ministering in their own local churches and visiting other local congregations. Since the first of this year it has been my privilege to be in many different churches for Bible conferences or supply preaching. As a result I have new inspiration and hope for Baptists as they take their tasks seriously where they are and through their gifts and prayers to the uttermost parts of the world.

The last of these visits for a Bible conference was with the people of the Temple Baptist Church in Owensboro. This is a relatively small congregation as city congregations go, but one with some of the biggest hearts and sincerest servants in the Lord's work.

Temple pastor Franklin Skaggs is as appreciative of the denomination and denominational workers as any pastor I know, but is first of all wedded to his flock and is attentive to all their needs. Consequently the love between a pastor and people at Temple for the eight years of Frank's ministry is something inspiring to behold.

And so here we are again where this editor has often ended up in conviction. The cutting edge and battle front for Baptists in this and all ages is the local congregation characterized by love for one another and for the world of lost people.

This means the denominational structure and programs exist for these churches and these churches exist for service to people. And so whether our calling as preacher or layman is to serve in denominational organizations or in local churches, it's a people-centered and love-motivated ministry if it is led by the spirit of the Living Lord. (April 24, 1971)

DALEY OBSERVATIONS ON HUMANITY

WESTERN RECORDER

KINDNESS IS STILL ALIVE AND DOING WELL

MUCH ABOUT THE MOOD AND THE SPIRIT OF today leads us to conclude regretfully that consideration, accommodation and kindness are forgotten virtues. It appears every man is for himself and the devil takes the hindmost.

We not only pay twice as much for gasoline but if we try to save a few pennies, we have to pump our gas, check the oil, the radiator, the battery and the pressure of our tires. Recently I went to three service stations before finding one with even self service air for tires.

But the milk of human kindness has not all dried up. I learned this on a recent Sunday when I was as much blessed by kindness from strangers as by the day's worship services.

It was one of those too-frequent Sunday mornings when proper Saturday preparation had not been made. My preaching appointment was many miles away and the gasoline tank was almost empty. Acting on the questionable theology of the ox being in the ditch, I pulled into a service station and waited on myself to the tune of $6.50. When I handed the young attendant a credit card he noticed it had expired. My total cash resources were $1 and only cash and one particular credit card could be accepted by the attendant.

The sole attendant was this young high school boy and both of us faced a crisis. He entered into my sufferings and agreed I could pay him the next day. He had never seen me, had no sure reason to believe me and took no security like a spare tire or my American Express card. He risked $6.50 of his own money on my word. My faith in human kindness was renewed and I hope this was strengthened when I drove 30 miles early Monday morning to pay him.

The end of that Sunday was more painful than the beginning, but it set my grateful heart to singing. On the return trip far from a garage or service station I heard a disturbing motor knock. Pulling off the road as soon as I could I discovered an engine hot as only an engine can be hot. I found a milk carton by the side of the road and a farm pond about a half mile away. My inclination first was to climb the fence and get water from the lake. A light in the nearby farm house persuaded me I had better ask before climbing the fence.

This way I met another complete stranger who was already in the bed. He not only gave me permission to have water but got up, dressed and brought a bucket of water from a nearby faucet. The radiator would not accept the water and obviously more was wrong. To make the story short, a half-hour later my car had been pulled up into the light from his garage, tools had been found by him and a stuck thermostat had been removed from the cooling system and the radiator filled. He refused to consider any pay and never knew I had but one dollar in my pocket.

Our conversation revealed he was a truck driver and had moved from Louisville to this farm with his wife and seven children. Furthermore he was a Roman Catholic and knew I was a Baptist preacher. I could not but wonder as he strained his muscles and burned his hands to help a Baptist preacher get home, how many Baptists including myself would have done as much for a Catholic priest.

One thing is certain. I arrived home with renewed confidence in humanity and the conclusion that the kindness of two strangers was a better sermon than I preached that day. (September 7, 1974)

HOSPITAL WALLS DO NOT A PRISON MAKE

FOR MANY YEARS ON VISITS TO THE KENTUCKY Baptist Hospital I passed by a closed door above which was written, "Department of Psychosomatic Medicine." I wondered what really went on behind this door. Since I did not know the truth I shared many of the misunderstandings and false notions which people have about emotional illness and its treatment.

Now I know how it feels to be behind this door. I have sat where the depressed sit and I have seen life through their eyes. I understand now why the Lord sent his prophet Ezekiel to sit speechlessly for seven days and nights with the Hebrew captives before he tried to minister to them. This is not to say the Lord sent me to the hospital. My illness was my own doing. I am confident, however, the Lord's mercy and love were evident in the provision of the hospital along with the doctors, the nurses and many others who constituted the healing team.

Emotional illness can wreck life for its victims, but it need not do so. Like all other human experiences which appear tragic, depression and its treatment can be redemptive instead of destructive. It depends upon how we respond to the illness and the available therapy.

How should one react when emotional illness comes and psychiatric care is needed? How does one escape the stigma

almost universally associated with mental illness? The first inclination is to conceal it and try to overcome it as quickly as possible
with the fewest friends possible knowing about it. Another temptation is to feel sorry for oneself and to complain about the
treatment from doctors, nurses and others trying to help.

Experience, however, has taught me that to face the situation
honestly and realistically and to cooperate completely with those
trying to help me is the only wise and sensible attitude.

I have learned that hospital walls — even the walls of a psychiatric ward — do not necessarily make a prison. Hospital walls and
strict regulations may make a prison for the body but not for the
spirit. The physical body can be restrained but neither space nor
time is a barrier for the human spirit which soars upon the wings
of inspired imagination and sacred meditation.

Friendship and fellowship are natural and meaningful among
partners in suffering. The usual barriers of age, sex, color and
social status are non-existent. My roommate who will ever be a
fast friend was a warm-hearted Hoosier. One of the most unforgettable characters for me was a young black of about 30 who
was everybody's friend.

There were three teenagers in the fellowship who demonstrated spiritual dimensions in a most interesting way. A dozen or
so of us usually ate lunch and supper together in the dining room
which doubled for an outpatient waiting room and a game room.
Understandably there are no planned religious services in the
psychiatric ward but it seemed natural to pause for a blessing
before we ate. After leading the prayer several times I learned that
the friendly 16-year-old lad wanted to say the blessing. At the next
meal he was invited to offer thanks for all of us. As we bowed he
began with the formula, "In the name of the Father, the Son and
the Holy Spirit," and continued with a beautiful, memorized
blessing. His prayer identified him as a Roman Catholic by faith
but his attitude identified him as a brother in spirit to all of us.

Next a beautiful 17-year-old girl let it be known that she would like to say the blessing sometime. When her time came her words were spontaneous and beautiful. They reflected her training in a Baptist Sunday school and a Christian home. For all of us mealtime came to be keenly anticipated for more than the food.

Trying to make some of the hours more meaningful I turned to Colossians to begin preparation for next January. Paul's prayer for the Colossians in the very first chapter became more understandable in light of my hospital experience. Paul besought for the Colossians the gifts of patience and long-suffering in their trials. To pray for such blessings seems proper but Paul asked for another blessing which seems contradictory. He asked for the Colossians joy in their tribulation. This joy is more than the stoical resignation to grin and bear hardships. It is true serenity conceived and born in suffering and which relates to fellow sufferers with cheerfulness and responds to God with thanksgiving. Such joyful serenity is as available in a hospital room as it is in the sanctuary because it is not an accomplishment of many but the gift of God. This is at least part of what Paul meant when he said "We know that in everything God works for good with those who love him." (November 10, 1973)

DISAGREEING IN LOVE

THERE IS A MUCH-NEEDED CHRISTIAN GRACE among Baptists today. This is the ability to disagree with each other on principles without letting it become a personal matter. We have given lip service to this precious trait, but have found it difficult to practice. Our failure has resulted in un-Christian conduct on the part of fellow church members and fellow Baptists in other relationships. Our Christian witness is dimmed and the world has reason to wonder if being a Christian makes any difference.

If this failure to respect and love each other while disagreeing were confined to young and immature Christians, it might be overlooked. Tragically, however, too many in high places of responsibility display the same littleness and pettiness. Occasionally it is out in the open; more often it is behind the scenes.

The ability to hold and express opposite convictions without personal feelings is basic to Baptist principles. Our belief in the competency of every individual to seek and discover God's will and the right of every individual to express himself demand that we allow for disagreement without taking personal offense.

There is a feeling in too many Baptist churches that one had better not disagree with the powers that be. By the powers that be is generally meant the pastor and the deacons. The fear is that to raise an objection to the "official" recommendation is to become a marked person.

Sometimes when this is claimed, it is not true. It is only the mistaken idea of some overly sensitive person. Regrettably, it is true sometimes and this is shameful. It is a sad day for Baptists when honest conviction cannot be expressed for fear of offending someone who has another opinion.

This doesn't mean that one must express himself on every matter just for the sake of airing his opinion. One who reacts to every proposal and expresses his private views without prayerfully seeking God's wisdom is a fool and a trouble-maker. However, one who remains silent, giving the impression he agrees when he actually disagrees is a hypocrite, and one who waits until after the meeting to mouth his disagreement is a coward.

No Baptist has the right to impose his conviction or opinion on any other Baptist. A person is completely out of place who feels that if you are not for what he is for, you are against him. It's a vain and overbearing person who says if you are his friend, you will support his position. Such a person is no friend to anyone, but rather views everyone as a tool to be used for self-advancement.

Human personality is the most precious thing in this world. Respect for human personality demands we give every person a right to his opinion without making it a personal matter. After all, no one has a corner on God's mind and any feeling of infallibility, no matter how important a person is, is completely out of place among Baptists. (May 27, 1965)

THE WORLD IS STARVING FOR LOVE

IN ANSWER TO A *WESTERN RECORDER* ARTICLE entitled "Myths About Ministers," a reader recently replied with a letter entitled "Myths About Laymen." What the letter writer said made a lot of sense to me. There was not only much truth in her words but also an undertone of hunger and longing between the lines.

This longing was for understanding, compassion and acceptance on the part of pastors for their sheep and for those not yet in the fold. By understanding is not meant indulgence or approval of wrong but a feeling that the man of God should know how perplexing are the problems of being a helpful parent, a faithful wife or husband, a sweet-spirited person in the face of mistreatment or an honest businessman in today's world. The desire of conscientious souls today is not to be told it's alright to go ahead and do what is obviously wrong but they do covet the understanding that someone knows how hard it is to resist evil when caught in the clutches of temptation.

Compassion is the ability to enter into another's suffering whether it is physical, emotional or spiritual. Compassion is more than a few oft-used ministerial words of assurance that if one turns it all over to Jesus, everything will be all right. It is more than a hurried prayer from a preacher making a dozen hospital calls in 45 minutes. It is actually entering into the experience of one who desperately needs the assurance that there is someone in addition to God who really cares.

Acceptance is likely the deepest longing of every soul. To be accepted for what he or she is—one made in the image of the Creator— as well as what one might be by the grace of God is a deep longing of every soul. This is the opposite of condemnation which never wins but always repels. The classic example is Jesus' treatment of the harlot caught in the act of her sin. The religionists of her day not only condemned her but were ready to kill her in the name of God. Jesus did not approve her behavior but was the one person on earth who really loved her enough to say, "I have nothing against you. Go and sin no more." I have an idea she found new life in his acceptance and forgiveness.

What does all this say? It says that whatever else we give to others as ministers or just disciples of Jesus we must give love. In loving one cannot call black white nor wrong right nor even deal in moral relativism but can speak the truth in love.

This love is not what is being sung about in the sentimental and lustful music of our day nor what is tried to be made respectable in X-rated movies. Nor even is it the warm friendliness which is far too scarce today. This loving is nothing else than the gift of self to one who doesn't deserve love by human standards. It is perfectly seen in the heart of God bleeding on the cross of Calvary for sinners.

This surely is the hardest of all gifts to give but it is the only truly redemptive gift in this world. And it is not possible to give it from purely human motivation but only when the one who first truly demonstrated it lives in us. The good news is that he will live in us if we dethrone self and we can love like he loved. This is the hope of the world. (February 5, 1972)

TWO JOURNEYS

THE AMAZING TRIP OF MAN TO THE MOON CALLS to mind another historic trip which was even more amazing and unbelievable. This was not man's journey from earth to the heavens but God's journey from heaven to earth.

Man's trip to the moon was measured in miles; God's journey to earth could be measured only in love and suffering.

Man's trip to the moon was planned in the minds of men only several years ago; God's journey to earth was planned in the heart of God from before the foundation of the earth.

Man's trip was made in a mechanical capsule; God's journey was made in human flesh.

Man announced his own arrival on the moon; the angels announced God's arrival on earth.

Man's trip to the moon cost millions of dollars; God's journey cost him his only Son.

Man had hope for escape from the moon and return to earth; there was no hope for God's Son to escape earth and return to heaven apart from dying on the cross.

Man's trip to the moon was only one of many space trips; God's journey to the earth in Jesus Christ was a once-for-all journey.

The moon trip freed man from earth; God's journey freed men from sin.

Future space trips of man will surely surpass this moon trip, but no journey of man will ever compare with the journey of God. The ascent of man will never equal the descent of God. Man is capable of human marvels; only God is capable of the divine miracle of the incarnation. (August 2, 1969)

DALEY OBSERVATIONS ON NATURE AND THE SEASONS

WESTERN RECORDER

FOR THE BIRDS

A VERY MATERNALLY-MINDED KILLDEER HAS chosen very holy ground for her nest this year. Selecting the parking lot of the Baptist Building at Middletown for her maternity ward, the beautiful ring-necked bird has hollowed out a nest in the loose gravel and laid four eggs which are almost the exact color of the limestone rocks of the parking lot.

I found her one day when I got out of my car, which was parked near her nest. She was fussing about the intrusion and puffed her feathers up to twice their normal size. She would not leave her nest except when almost pushed away and then not for much distance. Even an auto whose wheels straddled her nest later on did not deter her.

When approached by a human intruder, she first would voice her disapproval, then puff up her feathers and finally come off the nest toward the intruder with outstretched wings as if to attack, but carefully staying an arm's distance away.

The next day after finding her I went out to roll up the car windows as a June rain began to fall. Mrs. Killdeer was on her nest as usual and was undaunted by the first sprinkles. The rain, however, turned out to be a downpour and I tarried to watch this match between a prospective mother bird and the elements. As the rain continued, puddles formed around her, but she sat high and almost dry because she had chosen the highest spot of the area for her nest.

But then the rain continued as if the Lord of the clouds did not know of Mrs. Killdeer's problems. Her world became like that of Noah, only she had no ark. At first the water trickled into her nest but she didn't flinch. Gradually the water covered her eggs and then began to come up on her. At the height of the downpour only her head, neck and the top of her back were above the water but she stuck to her place.

As I sat and marveled at her faithfulness, I wondered what went through her bird mind. So far as I could tell not a word of complaint came from her about having it harder than other birds who nested in trees. She seemed to feel this was her job and she would stick to it. If, at the height of the storm, she considered her work was done and she should move elsewhere, she never revealed it. At last look, she was still on her nest and I'll predict before it's over something comes from it.

If this kind of faithfulness is for the birds, may the Lord increase the bird tribe! (June 22, 1961)

KENTUCKY IN THE SUMMERTIME

L IKE MARY IN THE MORNING OF THE CURRENTLY popular song, nothing is quite so lovely and beautiful as Kentucky in the summertime. Merely to be alive this time of year is to set the heart to singing and the soul to praising the Creator.

One of the many delights of denominational service is the privilege of traveling the length and breadth of our beautiful state. The variety and contrast of the Kentucky countryside are amazing. The mountains, covered with dark forests and in whose bosoms still lie huge deposits of black gold, remind one of the song of the psalmist, "I will lift up mine eyes unto the hills, from whence cometh my help."

The rolling Bluegrass country, with its crystal-clear streams and frolicking thoroughbreds, is more than legend claims. The knobs of Lincoln land with green hillsides and fertile fields make one wonder why the Lincolns ever left. And the flatlands of the river country of Western Kentucky, underlaid also with thick seams of coal, speak of plenty and prosperity.

Kentucky in the summertime also brings the hanging green beans, rosy red tomatoes, tender juicy corn and the other garden delights to be enjoyed now, and to be saved for tasty reminders of summer when the snow flies next winter. There is nothing so reassuring as full jars on pantry shelves, an overflowing cellar, corn in the crib, hay in the loft and a heart full of the Lord.

Summertime is also a holy time in Kentucky. The summer revival is still a great experience for many churches. Besides, there are church homecomings and anniversary celebrations by the score. Vacation Bible School and summer assemblies are a meaningful part of the summer for thousands of young people in Kentucky.

Summertime in Kentucky can also be a time of sharp contrast in weather. Often the clouds are few and far between, the sun shines too brightly upon my old Kentucky home and the thirsty roots of the forest and fields pray in vain for water. Again as this summer, the clouds are more than generous and pour destruction, as well as life, upon the earth.

The recent heavy rains have made for a sure harvest for early crops on high land, However, late corn and soybeans in bottom lands are in pathetic shape. Some fields along streams are in the water, while others are badly washed and eroded. In some places the weeds are as tall as the corn and beans, with the prospect for cultivation any time soon very dim.

Droughts and floods are religious problems for many humble folk of God. A deeply rooted belief is that God turns the rain on and off as reward or punishment upon those who live by the soil.

While it is true as the song says that he sends the sunshine and the rain, the harvest's golden grain, it is also true that he sends the rain upon the just and the unjust. It is better not to make the weather too much a theological matter, lest the result be perplexity and frustration.

In the weather, as in all other experiences of man, there is a mystery in the love of God. Everything that happens to good and bad men doesn't make sense as far as human reason goes. But faith in the Lord teaches us that favorable or unfavorable weather can make us stronger spiritually, for God does work all things for good to those who love him.

And who could but love him in Kentucky in the summertime? (July 20, 1967)

OCTOBER IN KENTUCKY

OCTOBER IN KENTUCKY IS AN EXHILARATING experience. It comes near being, if it is not actually, a religious experience. Kentucky autumn glory assures one that the God of creation had only beauty when he put together our magnificent land.

This is the year of years for nature's display of praise to God. The late rains added to the luxuriant growth of summer, making the foliage full and heavy for autumn's colors. The dogwoods began the parade with a scarlet red array of leaves that almost surpass the pink and white blossoms of May. Then came the sweetgums with another hue of red and the sycamores with their big rusty palms. Even the lowly sassafras has become a burning bush this October.

More glorious than any is the sugar maple. At first the color appears on the tips of the boughs as if some angelic paint crew went on a spraying spree. In the full dress parade the maples show off the yellow, gold, red and green all on the same tree. The strong oaks more slowly give up their green for red and brown before they reluctantly turn in for winter's sleep. The fantastic array of fall colors blended with the evergreens appears in the distance like a rainbow splattered against a Kentucky hillside.

Add to autumn's trees the crystal clear sunlight of October, the tender green grain of freshly sown fields, the fence rows of waving goldenrod and the sky blue streams singing their way through quiet meadows and limestone canyons and you have a picture that exceeds the imagination, surpasses the poet's words and defies the artist's brush. It can only be captured by the soul's eyes opened by the Creator of man and nature.

Can anything be added to the joy of an October drive or walk through the Kentucky countryside? Ah, yes, one experience remains to make it even more indescribable. This is to sit upon the crest of the crystal blue waters of Cumberland Lake at daybreak surrounded by autumn's hillsides reaching toward the morning stars and with a friend in the other end of the boat. The water's surface ripples with the gentle dawn breezes and the shallows along the rock shoreline bristle with activity of fish busy with their morning harvest. The gentle splash of the surface lure a few seconds hesitation by few life-like twitches. And then it happens! The water breaks. The lure disappears and the fight is on. Man against bass, what a thrill! It turns out to be one a fisherman dreams about. Out goes the line as he fights like a wild horse. Down to the bottom he goes determined to outwit his adversary and then to the surface to try to shake loose the hooks that hold him.

The heart beats like it's wild and the blood pressure runs away. Perspiration pops out and the whole body quivers with tension. Seconds seem like hours and minutes like days until the lunker gives up the fight and the landing net gently lifts him into the boat.

Such is October in Kentucky. It's worth more than a thousand vitamins and 10,000 tranquilizers. Heaven is not earth's happiest experiences as some poets say; but, if it were, Kentucky's October colors and Cumberland's dawn would be just inside the pearly gates. (October 28, 1965)

HOW TO BE THANKFUL

MOST LIKELY SOME READING THESE WORDS AT this moment are preparing for or recuperating from a traditional American Thanksgiving feast. After all, what would Thanksgiving be without the horn of plenty surrounded by a table heavily laden with turkey, old ham, oyster dressing, giblet gravy, mince meat pie, and all the accessories? A crackling fire in the fireplace, family members and friends gathered around, a football game in the afternoon, or some other favorite pastime make it just about a perfect day, or so we have come to think.

Our celebration today must be a far cry from the first Thanksgivings of our Pilgrim fathers. In their place we would consider we had nothing to be thankful for; in our places they would be lost as to where to start to celebrate for even the feasts of those hard colonial days would not appear as a feast compared to our bounties today.

What is the true spirit of Thanksgiving? Does it depend upon what we have or what we are? It's all according to our philosophy of life. If the main purpose of life is to get everything we want, to be fat, full and happy all the time, and satisfy every bodily appetite, then laden tables, warm fires and admiring friends are necessities. If, on the other hand, the purpose of life is to make us strong and mature, to grow in grace and to give ourselves in sacrificial living, then material things don't count too much.

These philosophies are illustrated in two men in the New Testament who uttered expressions of thanksgiving. One man, after a bountiful year and a heavy harvest, summed up his thanksgiving spirit with these words, "Soul, thou hast much goods laid up for many years; take thine ease, eat, drink and be merry" (Luke 12:19).

The other man's harvest had been a little different. Things he had gathered included labors more abundant, stripes above measure, frequent prisons, deaths oft, five floggings of 40 stripes save one, three beatings with rods, one stoning, three shipwrecks, a day and a night in the deep, journeys often, perils of waters, perils of robbers, perils by his own countrymen, perils by heathen, perils in the city, perils in the wilderness, perils in the sea, perils among the false brethren, weariness and painfulness, hunger, thirst, fasting, cold and nakedness. With this harvest Paul came to his Thanksgiving Day with this testimony and with this invitation, "In everything give thanks! For this is the will of God in Christ Jesus concerning you" (1 Thessalonians 5:18).

If our attitude in life is that of the fool in the parable of Jesus, suffering, hardship and want have no place. But if we share

Paul's philosophy, these things are only part of the everything for which we are to give thanks.

The early Pilgrims' thanksgiving had more in common with that of Paul; ours generally is more like that of the fools in the parable of Jesus.

The rigors of the New England winter along with the diseases and the savages of the wilderness built a sturdiness and virility in our forefathers that gave us our greatness. What is our way of life building that can be given to coming generations? It's a sobering thought for this Thanksgiving Day. (November 26, 1959)

WHAT'S GOOD ABOUT CHRISTMAS?

IS THERE ANYTHING LEFT IN CHRISTMAS THAT IS good? With so many elements of our Christmas that were completely unknown to the Babe of Bethlehem, sometimes we wonder if our observance is not more pagan than Christian. Crass commercialism, unpaid shopping bills, exchange of gifts through obligation, liquid celebrating, unholy office parties and such make many wish Christmas was over before it started.

Poor old Christmas! Exploited by business, prostituted by revelers and decried by preachers! Is there no one with a kind word for Christmas in our day?

With all that is bad about our modern celebrations, there's still a lot that is good about Christmas.

The lowest level of Christian meaning is the good cheer of the holiday season. Granted this is all some get out of it, which is far too little, it is still worthwhile. The end of every year would be drab indeed without lighted Christmas trees, holly wreaths, Santa and his reindeer, colorful greeting cards and family gatherings.

Gaiety, gladness and children's laughter have a place in this world that so often brings burdens and loneliness to so many.

Whom besides the Lord of eternal life should one think of at Christmas more than friends and a mother or a father through whom came physical life? What warms the heart more than the warm flickers of the old family fireplace or satisfies the deepest hunger more than mother's Christmas table? Those fortunate enough to have parents living should enjoy the good cheer of Christmas with them. "I'm Dreaming of a White Christmas" and "I'll Be Home for Christmas" are not religious carols but they speak a universal language and express a human need deeper than shallow superficiality.

Beyond the good cheer of Christmas is the good will of Christmas first announced by the angels. Eagerly greeted by the Judean shepherds, the good will of heaven extended to man in the manger meets a human hunger not satisfied with mere good cheer. Men and nations alike who experience goodwill and express it to each other are pleasing to God now as they were when the angels first announced the coming of his Son. Christmas generally brings the best of men to the surface and helps hope spring eternally that goodwill some time will be the will of all men.

By far the best of Christmas is the good news it proclaims. Good cheer and goodwill are both hollow apart from the meaning they receive from the good news, and without the good news of the manger we have never really known Christmas nor come all the way to Bethlehem. The tragedy is that starting toward Christmas so many of us stop short of the star and attending the feast, we never come to know the Host.

Simply put, the good news is that One came from heaven to be our Savior from sin, our Light and Darkness, our Guide in the earthly pilgrimage. This good news set the angels to singing, the shepherds to praising and the wise men to searching.

With all that's bad about it, there's still a lot that's good about Christmas. Let's not miss any of the good this year. (December 24, 1959)

ON A WINTER MORNING

ON A WINTER MORNING STARS IN THE PREDAWN
darkness appear like jagged holes in the sky through which
the light of fire beyond comes. The chill of the winter air makes
one tingle from head to feet. A walk down a wooded trail in the
darkness is easier than it seems and a seat on the ground against
a cedar is almost like going back to bed.

The first gray in the eastern horizon appears, but still there
are no signs of life except the occasional crowing of a rooster on
a distant farm. Then from an overhead bough comes a sound of a
waking bird. He is unaware any human has invaded his world.

Suddenly all of the sounds are overshadowed by the low
cluck of wild ducks coming off their roost in bushes along the
creek. Then in the gray darkness their graceful forms glide upon
the water as they move out in search for breakfast. They are soon
out of sight but reveal their location with an occasional quack.

A few feet away the weeds stir and the leaves rustle. Then a
sleek, beautiful striped little chipmunk appears within arm's
reach. He, too, can't distinguish the still human form from a
stump or a log leaning against the cedar tree.

Even a wood mouse gets into the early morning activity as he
comes out of his warm bed to do his early foraging. Across the
creek a squirrel barks and meows like a cat. From a nearby tree
he is answered by another bushy tail. Perched gracefully upon a
limb, his arched tail has a little jerk for every bark.

A gentle splash on the creek's far edge turns out to be a
muskrat. He's an expert fisherman and soon will have his daily
quota. He splits the water as he moves gracefully across the creek
and leaves a trail in the water like a snake.

The creek water, warm from the recent rains, is alive with life.
Even the fish are playful though it's the middle of winter.

The first rays of the sun come like a gleaming arrow through
the trees. The bold activity of the creatures of nature diminishes

with the brightness of advancing day.

What's it all about? It's an editor on a Saturday morning, finding soul refreshment in the world of nature and a challenge in pursuit of the clever wild duck.

The sounds of God's world of nature on an early winter morn along a beautiful creek in Kentucky—is there anything to compare with it? (January 9, 1965)

SPRING RAIN IN THE CUMBERLANDS

AMONG HUMAN EXPERIENCES THERE ARE FEW as moving as Kentucky's Cumberland Mountains in April. The experience is heightened during a spring rain in the mountains. There's a mysterious majesty about the lightening that electrifies the peaks and the thunder which echoes across the valleys. The fields and forests welcome the pouring of heaven's blessings and absorb liquid reservoirs for the growth of coming days.

The falling rain upon newly turned soil makes rivulets which cut murky ribbons across the fields which were cleared long years ago from the forests by pioneers. These were hardy souls who gave up the tidewater lands of the East for the adventure of the mountainous terrain of the West. In an April shower the farm animals do not retreat to shelter but continue to munch the tender green pasture-land grass while enjoying the warm bath.

The whole earth, and especially the woodland, is aglow with spring colors. Dogwood like suspended snowflakes make brilliant bouquets among the dark mountain pines. Lacking the symmetry of their domestic unshaded fellows, the wild dogwoods are made more beautiful by their struggle with taller trees for life-giving sunbeams and raindrops.

The forests present an unbelievable variety of shades and colors of newly appearing leaves. The tiny, almost colorless oak leaves of April give no hint of their rich July green and their October brown. Yet the roots of the oaks are taking hold of the water and minerals of the earth as a saint's roots reach for the depths of God's love.

Raindrops fall from the small tender spring leaves with their sleepy sound upon last winter's bed of leaves. Thunder of the passing storm rumbles across the sky like the sound of God's voice trying to escape earth, one room of the universe. Underneath feet that seem shoeless on holy ground before a burning bush, violets make a purple carpet snuggling close to the earth's womb from which they so recently were born.

Mountain birds twitter between raindrops and continue their search for straw and twigs in preparation for the universal venture of romance and reproduction.

A brightly attired woodpecker watches the intruder with one eye as he rings with the perfection of a geometry teacher the trunk of an apple tree with a circle of holes. From the mountaintop misty eyes view billowy rain-emptied clouds below which cling to the mountainsides like burned incense reluctant to rise to God.

The heavens declare the glory of God and the firmament shows his handiwork. So do the Cumberlands in an April rain. What a world! What a Creator! (May 12, 1966)

DALEY OBSERVATIONS ON EDUCATION

WESTERN RECORDER

BETHEL COLLEGE IS IN HARD WAY

BETHEL COLLEGE IN HOPKINSVILLE IS IN A HARD way. Prospects which have not been overly bright for several years have been less encouraging of late. And now the college is definitely in a crisis.

There are several problems which contribute to Bethel's dilemma. Enrollment is one of these. About 200 seems to be the number of students Bethel has been able to attract, and this is not enough. Enrollment is related to facilities and curriculum, and in both of these respects Bethel has been limited. Trying to get along mainly with one major building which is outmoded and a limited campus, the school has not been able to attract many boarding students. The commuting students have passed up Bethel mostly for other schools where a wider variety of courses are offered. Another problem for Bethel is finances. Bethel has been hard-pressed financially like all other Baptist schools in Kentucky, but even more so. The increase in the number of four-year Baptist colleges in Kentucky with the resultant change in the fund distribution formula has squeezed Bethel into a hard place.

Efforts to raise money in special fund-raising campaigns have not been too successful. A campaign several years ago raised enough to pay the expenses. An all-out campaign last year was moderately successful but fell short of the goal and failed to avert the present crisis.

The conclusion of the matter is that Bethel has done a good job for the resources with which she has had to work. The limited facilities, low enrollment and inadequate finances have inevitably led to the present crisis. Plans for the opening of a University of Kentucky two-year branch college in Hopkinsville in 1965 do not make the Bethel picture brighter but rather darker.

What is to happen to Bethel? The administration and trustees are saying the successful continuation of the school in Hopkinsville is not possible. Two alternatives are left. The school can be relocated or discontinued.

Presently the trustees are open for offers of other communities in Western Kentucky for the relocation of Bethel. So far no offer of the magnitude needed to relocate a college has been announced.

One thing is certain and this is indeed fortunate. The Bethel College board of trustees is made up of some of the strongest, ablest and wisest Baptists in Kentucky. They can be trusted to take all the facts into consideration and make recommendations in keeping with the best interest of Bethel College and Kentucky Baptists.

A praise-worthy attitude in the matter has been taken by the Baptist leadership in the Hopkinsville area. Selfishness and sectionalism which are the natural reactions in most instances like this were completely put aside when the Christian County Baptist Association Executive Board passed resolutions encouraging the Bethel administration and trustees in their efforts to find another location for a greater Bethel. (January 9, 1964)

BETHEL TRUSTEES DESERVE COMMENDATION

THE TRUSTEES OF BETHEL COLLEGE DESERVE the understanding and gratitude of Kentucky Baptists. History reveals that the closing of a Baptist college is an extremely delicate and difficult matter. Reason and wisdom are often overruled by sentiment and emotion.

Not so in the case of the Bethel trustees. The going has been difficult for a number of years at Bethel. The trustees have made valiant efforts to keep life and health in the institution. They also gave ample opportunity for anyone interested in providing for the future of the college to come forth.

At the same time the administration and the faculty members have been unselfish and sacrificial beyond reasonable expectation.

Now the inevitable has been faced. Institutions like individuals serve their time, and it is not necessary that every college live forever any more than a man is to live forever on this earth.

Having served well, Bethel's day for passing is here, however sad it be. Instead of prolonging the misery by administering financial glucose in the face of the inevitable end, why not have an honorable ending and a fitting memorial service?

Any other course would appear irresponsible. To sit by and let the assets of Bethel, built up at great sacrifice through the years, be eaten up completely by heavy deficit operations would not be keeping good faith with Kentucky Baptists of this or earlier generations. Let us hope that, faced with similar circumstances, those responsible for administering other Baptist institutions will be as responsible and wise as the Bethel College trustees. (March 3, 1964)

A DECISIVE DAY IN HISTORY

OCTOBER 9, 1960, COULD WELL BE THE MOST decisive day in this century for Baptists in the Louisville area. This the day set for a ground-swell of expression of loyalty and pledge of support to Kentucky Southern College.

Just 150 years ago Baptists in America were unorganized, highly individualistic, mostly suspicious of each other and relatively weak. They had many virtues but had not learned to work together. But God moved in a mysterious way to change this. Two missionaries, Adoniram Judson and Luther Rice, sent out by another religious group, discovered upon arriving upon their mission field that both, through individual and separate study of the New Testament, had become Baptists.

This was some predicament. Two missionaries who were Baptists were on a foreign mission field but there was no Baptist organization of any kind in all of America to sustain and support them. Being a wise man, Judson knew that Baptists could not enter the foreign mission enterprise without missionary organizations back home to provide support for those on the field and without schools in which to train those whom God called to go. Consequently, Judson stayed on the mission field while Rice was sent back to America to fan the flames of mission in the hearts of Baptists.

And what a job Rice did! Through his efforts the Triennial Convention of Baptists was formed in Philadelphia in 1814 for the explicit purpose of supporting the foreign mission movement. Rice also traveled all over the eastern section of the United States pleading for education, and Baptist schools and colleges sprang up all over the land. Since that day of beginnings hundreds of thousands of Baptist young people have been trained for mission service in Baptist schools.

Kentucky has followed this early pattern of Baptist organization and education. Today the General Association embodies more than 2,300 Baptist churches and more than 600,000 Baptists. Four colleges, a Bible school and a Baptist high school are supported by Kentucky Baptists today.

The largest concentration of Baptists in Kentucky is in Louisville. With the steady growth of the Baptist witness in the Louisville area, it was inevitable that a Baptist college would be needed and wanted in the Louisville area. Surveys showed that a Baptist college was long overdue in Louisville. The first formal move was in 1956 when the General Association approved with enthusiasm an action of the Long Run Association calling for the establishment of a school by Louisville Baptists. The initiative in securing a suitable location and erecting adequate buildings with which to begin the school was left to the Louisville area.

Remarkable progress has been made in four years and Kentucky Southern College already has extremely valuable assets. The spacious and beautiful campus, already being developed on Shelbyville Road, could hardly be matched in America for strategic and valuable location. The first building, the president's home, has been completed and is already occupied.

In this president's home is the man undoubtedly sent by God for the hour. Few men have ever given up so much to accept by faith such a challenge, and few men have ever brought such high qualifications for an assignment. When Dr. Rollin S. Burhans resigned the pastorate at Crescent Hill Baptist Church to become president of the new Louisville college, many who were somewhat doubtful about the success of the project became persuaded that this dream would now become a reality. Like Abraham of old, who left comfortable Ur for a land yet unseen, Rollin Burhans left one of the best pastorates in the Southern Baptist Convention for the dream of a Baptist college in Louisville. The new president has clear convictions of what a Baptist college ought to be and brings to the college the best qualifications a president could possess. He is literally laying his life on the line with faith in God and in the prayers and gifts of fellow Baptists.

Another asset of the new college is the intense interest of several Baptist benefactors like the Cookes and the Highbaughs. These families are in position to help the school get started, and their deposition in this direction is valuable beyond estimate. All in all Kentucky Southern College has about as many assets as such an institution could expect to possess in such a short period of time.

What else is needed? One all-important thing has yet to come if Kentucky Southern College is to move from the dream stage of reality. This is an expression of universal acceptance and support by Louisville Baptists. All successful Baptist projects are movements of the Baptist masses. The enthusiasm and support of a few leaders or all the pastors, for that matter, are not sufficient. Kentucky Southern College must be the concern of all of us.

A college of the type in the mind of President Burhans is a tremendous undertaking. The magnitude of the project is not easily realized. It is not to result from the generosity of only several people and the dedication of a president but the sacrifices of many and dedication for years to come.

This is why next Sunday is all-important. If 30,000 to 40,000 Louisville Baptists will indicate their future support of the college by making some gift on this Sunday, even if it be only a token gift, President Burhans will be a long way through the wilderness toward the promised land. There are few Baptist families in Louisville which could not provide at least one honorary founder or alumnus of Kentucky Southern.

Louisville Baptist churches and pastors should not pass up this historic opportunity to let their members have a part in this once-in-a-lifetime project. History will recall a telling record of this day. Churches with building debts or other local projects will not lose by urging their members to be generous toward Kentucky Southern. Surely no pastor or finance committee or group of deacons will fail to give utmost cooperation in this matter.

The need of Kentucky Southern is proven. Many have said, "We're for it." Neither is there any doubt about our ability to build a great Baptist school in Louisville. The only question that remains is, "Will we?" Next Sunday will go a long way in telling.

As editor of the *Western Recorder* I only wish I could convey my deep feeling in this matter. I taught five years at Georgetown College and saw firsthand the ministry of this great Baptist school. I don't believe any money spent by Kentucky Baptists will mean more for what Baptists are called to do than that spent in Christian education.

I watch the campus at Kentucky Southern almost every day. I never pass by without a surge in my heart and one of the happiest days in my life will be when the first students enter a Kentucky Southern classroom.

The easiest pledge I ever made was for a monthly contribution to this college dream when the first drive for funds was made. Every month since then my little check has gone to this dream and will continue to do so. I hope to be only one of thousands who will experience this joy after the decisive day of October 9. (October 6, 1960)

A SAD BUT WISE SEPARATION

IN A TRULY HISTORIC ACTION AT BOONE LODGE on March 10, 1967, Kentucky Baptists and Kentucky Southern College took a step that might prove to be the way Baptists in other states will approach the severe problems of higher education today. The denomination and the college parted ways in a friendly manner with the denomination providing $885,000 to help the college in its transition from a church-related to an independent college.

In one way it is surprising that Kentucky Baptists, long known for their conservative approach toward change, took such a novel step. Though not the last to lay the old aside, we have rarely been the first for which the new is tried. But special circumstances which led Kentucky Southern to ask severance from the convention afforded the convention with the opportunity to be a trailblazer.

President Rollin Burhans is to be highly commended for his candid, sincere and complete appraisal of the present financial plight of the college. He is to be admired for sticking to his dream for the school to the point of literally giving himself. The Executive Board members responded with concern, under-standing and disposition to do all possible to help the school. Only great concern for other Kentucky Baptist causes, world-wide mission causes and the continued good spirit and response of Kentucky Baptists to the Cooperative Program prevented board members from doing more for the school.

The action of the Executive Board in releasing Kentucky Southern College from convention control and in giving the school $885,000 to help relieve its critical financial crisis is wise, fair and mutually advantageous to the school and the convention. For the school it affords a chance to survive as a quality college by finding other financial help including government loans and grants. For the Kentucky Baptist Convention it will give some relief in the years ahead from an unbearable financial load in higher education.

Kentucky Southern deserves to live. It is already an institution of superior academic quality. It has one the highest academically qualified faculties of any Baptist college in the Southern Baptist Convention. The students who are there love the school and praise it. The school can be just as Christian as an independent, private college as it could be as a Baptist school.

The Kentucky Baptist Convention has several reasons for reacting favorably to the request from Kentucky Southern to be released and for giving financial help to the school. The college expressly said it did not want to come into the convention before it was academically and financially strong. However, when the Christian Education Campaign was launched, it was highly desirable that a united front be presented and so Kentucky Southern agreed reluctantly to come in. Their share of the $9 million goal was to be $2 million. The failure of the statewide drive to come anywhere near the goal resulted in Kentucky Southern getting only about $200,000 for capital needs.

In the meantime the new school, without buildings and other resources of established schools, felt it had to proceed with buildings and other requirements for accreditation even without the certainty of income from the denomination. This gamble didn't pay off and this is at least part of the cause of the school's present plight. So far Kentucky Southern has most likely lost more than she has gained financially by coming into the convention. Therefore, it is only fair that the convention help her to the extent of the convention's present financial ability and in line with her commitments.

The releasing of Kentucky Southern is an economy move for the convention, at least in the long run. It is clear now that Kentucky Baptists are not committed enough to Baptist higher education to afford four senior colleges and two other schools. It can only be viewed as wise to lighten our educational load and eventually free finances for schools that remain or for other mission purposes.

The releasing of Kentucky Southern College will serve to reduce some friction and controversy in the convention over how schools are to be financed and over other school policies. Kentucky Southern and other Baptist schools that survive with strength will ultimately have to take government loans and even government grants and this will be controversial among Baptists for many years to come.

In leaving the Baptist fold, Kentucky Southern should be constrained to remain the kind of school Kentucky Baptists can be proud of having been a part and will continue to be a part on an individual basis. Let us hope this step gives Kentucky Southern a new lease on life and that a good school stands to become a great school. Kentucky Baptists can ever live without regret for having made a significant contribution toward the realization of a dream and for helping make a school that might well serve Baptists better in the future than in the past. (March 16, 1967)

WHAT MEANS THIS THING?

THE RECENT CONTROVERSY AT SOUTHERN Seminary that resulted in the dismissal of 13 professors is the Baptist story of the year and very well could be the Baptist story of the 20th century. Only one of the dismissed professors, J.J. Owens, sought and obtained reinstatement. The others held that since the intolerable conditions which they described in their report have not been changed, they have no desire to continue their relationship with the seminary and even refused to talk with the reinstatement committee of the trustees.

The question now becomes, "What is the meaning of this incident for these professors, for the seminary and for Southern Baptists?"

The history of Christianity is full of such incidents. In nearly every case such incidents are soon forgotten. They become only a paragraph in a history book and have little permanent effect on the life of the faith in which they occur. However, in some instances they have been epoch making and have changed the whole course of Christian history. They have produced major changes in the life of a denomination and, in some cases, have even been the beginning of a new denomination.

Which is this incident? Is it only a slight stirring of the waters soon to subside as the waves from a pebble thrown into a stream or is it the beginning of a tempest to disturb deeply or even radically change Baptist waters? There may be those among us wise enough to predict the future effects of this incident upon Baptist life, but they are also likely wise enough not to express themselves. This editor is not likely wise enough in either respect.

What will be the effect of their dismissal upon the professors and their future ministry? This is a critical matter. Inevitably they will be judged. First, their method of protest will be questioned. Even if it is granted that they had just grievances, did they act wisely in presenting a document critical of the president and his administration and presenting it in such a way that, to the trustees, it came to be a matter of a choice between them and the president? Will their banding together, which intentionally or unintentionally had the effect of a power bloc, be judged as right or wrong? Should they have resigned separately or together in protest rather than holding out for a censure of the president? How many will agree with their claim that this was their only course?

Second, once they had expressed their convictions, and the president was officially upheld and reconciliation was invited, was principle or pride involved in their refusal to be reconciled? Many Baptists will say principle and many others will insist it was pride. Others will say both and only history will finally answer the question.

An important question now is what will happen to these men. Will they suffer an unofficial ban by Southern Baptists or will they quickly be offered places of service commensurate with their ability? The most regrettable outcome possible would be that these men and their contributions to Southern Baptist life be lost or minimized. As men of conviction they should be considered like many other Baptists who have chosen not to serve under certain circumstances. They should be treated like any Baptist pastor who has been dismissed from the church he served because of principle and personality conflicts.

The subsequent behavior of these men will go a long way in determining the sincerity and rightness of their action. If they should become agitators and dissension-makers for the seminary and the denomination, their claim as Christian men acting upon principle will be seriously questioned. Several of the professors who have expressed themselves insist they were mistreated in being dismissed but that they hold no malice toward anyone and only want to continue their ministry in some God-directed place. Treatment by fellow Baptists should be such as to make possible this desire.

Dr. William Morton is joining the new Midwestern Seminary faculty. Others of the group could well be used in other Baptist seminaries and colleges. All of these men are good preachers and could be used of God mightily in pastorates. If any of these men happen to continue their ministry in non-Baptist churches or schools, it should be a result of their deliberate choice, not due to any mistreatment from fellow Southern Baptists. Love destroyed by differences in thinking is less than Christian.

Of serious concern is the effect of the rift upon the seminary. Any way it is viewed and any way it might be used of God for good in the future, the seminary is temporarily seriously crippled.

This sacrosanct institution of nearly a century of service to Southern Baptists has been held in great respect and almost in awe by its thousands of graduates and many other Baptists. That such a thing could happen to Southern Seminary was unthinkable even when it began to appear inevitable. Now the bubble is burst and it's just another institution. No matter how divine its significance, it has suffered at the hands of human frailties and whatever smugness we have displayed as alumni ought to be replaced with repentance and humility.

Certainly many who never felt the seminary needed her alumni now know better. Doubtless many of us who never seriously prayed for the seminary have added her to the priority list. Of all the needy hours of Southern's history, none is more critical than this.

Can the faculty be rebuilt? Can sagging morale be restored? What about enrollment in the next few years? Can the present student body be held together? These are real questions.

Of course the faculty can be rebuilt, but it will be a tremendous task. Care and caution must be exercised. Known for unusual quality of scholarship and devotion, this faculty must be preserved as such. Many qualified men would have to take a salary cut to join the faculty if the present salary scale is maintained. Others would not be available upon such short notice.

What about the morale of the faculty members left? The tension became such that almost everyone had to take sides. Having done so, have necessary independence and freedom been preserved? Will new faculty members as well as old ones feel they are given notice by the recent trustee decision to cooperate without raising questions? Can the president escape serious injury from the charges even though vindicated?

It appears that the remaining faculty members are characterized by such a high morale that it is described as a spiritual revival. A tremendous load falls upon them and there is every sign that they will rise to the occasion.

Students are known to be ready to take sides and they have. Other individuals and churches have also. My desk is already filled with letters of support on both sides.

Two observations might be made concerning the future of the seminary.

First, the academic freedom of the classroom within unwritten but understood bounds must be maintained. The use of all tools of modern research has produced intellectual responsibility for the seminary which is invaluable. Presentation of all views on theological issues has distinguished the seminary from so called "Bible schools" where only one view is taught and tolerated. What has happened must not change this.

In the second place, the role of the seminary in the life of Baptists must be clearly understood. This has not been so. Southern Baptists and their seminary faculties have not always clearly understood what they expected of each other. Maybe this has been the fault of both.

One result of the episode may be a clarification of the direction of future theological training in our other seminaries as well as at Southern. Whatever else is expected of a Southern Baptist seminary, the majority of Baptists expect it to produce preachers of evangelistic, warm-hearted passion as well as scholars of intellectual acumen. Men are expected to come out of seminary classes with love and devotion to the Bible and ability to present its good news as well as to discuss all its critical problems. They are to love dearly their denomination as well as see its faults, and are to engage conscientiously and energetically in its world mission. Our seminaries are to be primarily schools of prophets, not producers of intellectual giants. We need giants but we probably will go on using available privately endowed and state-supported schools of divinity for their training.

Who can say what the incident will mean to the denomination? The episode forces us to re-examine the principle of freedom as Baptists interpret it. Why did these men feel threatened? Was it imaginary or real? Are we experiencing normal growing pains as a denomination or is it that we simply must give up traditional procedures with growth and necessary delegation of responsibility to committees and boards that once were assumed by the whole body. In short, the question is, can we become big and efficient without losing our democracy? We can, but only by carefully avoiding known pitfalls of centralization, control and conformity.

The incident also should at least lead Baptists to examine the administrative structure of our institutions. Do we have inherent weaknesses in our institutional setup that tend to develop tension between administration and staff or faculty? This is not the only seminary where serious tension has developed, and mortal conflict between college administrations and faculties has been and is all too common. We might need to do some defining and delineating. Again as Baptists, we must come again by this event to understand the price of a denomination free from constituted authoritarian control. Many have expressed disappointment that this thing happened. This is understandable. Some have expressed disappointment that it could happen. This is lamentable.

Finally we must confess that the all-important matter is the character and spirit of our souls; not the system under which we operate. With the right spirit most any system will work; with the wrong spirit, hardly any system will suffice. At this point, we could all well think of spiritual revitalization. We speak of community revival and church revival. We might do well to think of denominational revival which would begin with nine million Southern Baptists on the mourner's bench. (July 24, 1958)

SING ONE SONG FOR CARVER

A TINGE OF SADNESS COMES OVER THE HEARTS of many Southern Baptists near and far with the announcement of the proposed merger of Carver School of Missions and Social Work with the Southern Baptist Theological Seminary.

Some of the sadness is sentimental of course. Thousands of former students and hundreds of thousands of Southern Baptist Woman's Missionary Union ladies will never forget the Woman's Missionary Training School and its thrilling beginning under the influence mostly of William Owen Carver, for whom the school was very appropriately later named. It was formally inaugurated in 1907 at exercises in the Broadway Baptist Church, though some young ladies had already been unofficially enrolled in Southern Seminary for missionary training.

The beautiful building at 334 East Broadway used by the Training School from 1907 until 1941, when the new campus on Lexington Road adjacent to Southern Seminary was occupied, is still pointed out to Baptist sightseers in Louisville. The Training School became Carver School of Missions and Social Work in 1953, and in 1956 the ownership and control of the school was changed from Woman's Missionary Union to the Southern Baptist Convention.

Another sentimental consideration is the history of romance between the seminary men and the Training School ladies. The picturesque and romantic valley separating the campuses has been the scene of many daytime, non-academic conversations and nighttime, moonlight strolls of destiny. It was called the Valley of Decision and there were even remarks that some of the ladies gave more than ordinary encouragement to the decisions, but everybody really knew better. At least many a shy, reluctant and unattached preacher-boy found attachment, a mate and his strength in this valley, and not a few unclaimed jewels changed their destiny from the foreign mission field to a Southern Baptist pastorium in the same valley.

But enough of sentiment! At that I'm speaking vicariously, for I had been in the valley several years before my seminary days began.

Why is Carver School in its last days as a separate institution? It now appears the year 1962-63 will be Carver's last year.

President Nathan Brooks and the Carver trustees have tried valiantly to maintain the school for a valuable function in the Southern Baptist life. Only when faced with insurmountable difficulties have they proposed merger.

President Brooks has put it on the line. The school cannot be accredited for training professional social workers, and enrollment, which was already too low, is declining even more. In 1959 when the convention decided to continue the school after receiving it from Woman's Missionary Union in 1956, there were good reasons to expect to receive accreditation for Carver as a school for professional social work training. Now the accreditation association not only has refused to recognize the school as such, but holds no hope for such recognition under the present plan of operation.

President Brooks and the Carver trustees did not give up easily. They have explored possibilities of merging with a college, which is part of the requirements of accreditation. They were not successful. They approached the Foreign Mission Board and the Home Mission Board for possible connections and were not encouraged. They have turned to Southern Seminary as the best hope for continuing the present program and ideals of Carver. They hope some identity of the school, including the name, can be preserved.

The proposed merger is by no means certain. It will be considered by Southern Seminary trustees in their annual meeting this month. If approved, the matter would go to the Executive Committee of the Southern Baptist Convention and eventually to the convention itself for approval.

There are many in the Convention who believe strongly that Southern Baptists should have at least one school to train professional social workers. Only such professionally trained workers can qualify for many positions, and Roman Catholics have something of a corner on such training today.

The proposed merger of Carver with Southern would not provide professional training. It is hoped, however, some Carver scholarships might be available for Baptist students who might be interested in going from the seminary to schools accredited for professional social training.

Whatever the outcome for Carver, let this be said for President Brooks and the Carver trustees: They faced the facts and made a recommendation in keeping with them. This is in sharp contrast with the usual attitude of those with vested interests who fight to keep whatever Baptist support they can get whatever the facts about the agency or institution might be. (March 8, 1962)

SCHOOL DAYS AGAIN

NEVER A SEPTEMBER APPROACHES THAT I DON'T relive boyhood days. Somehow back there it didn't take much to thrill a youngster.

About this time of year we looked longingly at all the pretty things in the mail-order catalog and sent off the order for school clothes. It had to be cash then which was hard to come by, but it still had its advantages over the easy-to-come-by-but-hard-to-pay-for credit card system today.

In about four or five days we began watching for the mail carrier. When he finally put the package in the mailbox, it was some thrill to open it to see your fall wardrobe. The fact that other boys and girls had their clothes ordered from the same catalog and often got identical garments made no difference.

The first day of school was a real event. Usually there were new teachers to see and try out. There was the scramble for back or front desk according to whether you wanted to have fun or make grades.

Then there was the smell of new overall pants which now youngsters think have to be laundered before wearing. Added to every other discomfort of returning to school was the indescribable burning feet in shoes after a summer of barefooted bliss.

Like most other experiences of life, school days appear more important in retrospect than when we are actually going to school. We try to lecture our children on the importance of school but they are slow to hear. But not even children can live in our world today without knowing that training is absolutely imperative.

Millions of young Americans are off to school these days. These are all the way from first-graders to college and graduate school enrollees. Some of us who have been there could tell these some helpful things if they would only listen.

Here are several suggestions especially for those going to college:

1. Choose the right companions. You are on your own in the choice of your company and not everyone you meet at college is uplifting. The right companion is as important as the right courses.

2. Maintain your religious habits. Again there is not mother or father to urge church attendance and the temptation not to go is great. Your spiritual growth is as important as your intellectual development. Daily scripture reading and prayer cannot be left off without tragic results.

3. Take the hard courses in stride. Don't put off the rough ones until later and don't look for crip courses. There are some but you pay your money for quality education. College education without foreign language and laboratory science is like salt without savor.

4. Avoid psuedo-intellectualism. Beware of the professor who delights in destroying your simple religious faith without

replacing it with a more mature one. Deal with your doubts honestly but hold to your faith while dealing with doubt. According to the best biblical scholars and best scientists there is no irreconcilable conflict between an enlightened understanding of the Bible and the best of modern science.

5. Mix study with recreation, not recreation with study. There is one thing worse than not taking any exercise at all and this is taking exercise all the time. A strong mind in a strong body requires a proper balance between physical and mental activities.

6. Take full advantage of the Baptist Student Union. This organization will help tremendously in all the matters mentioned above.

7. Remember always you are on you own. You'll have to make your own decisions, and success or failure will be mostly your own personal responsibility.

Oh, yes, I almost forgot. If you are among the young people who have a car, leave it at home. You'll come nearer being a college graduate driver sometime. (August 31, 1961)

DALEY OBSERVATIONS ON
RELIGION AND THEOLOGY

THERE IS MUCH RIGHT WITH THE CHURCH TODAY

IN A DAY WHEN THE PREVAILING PREOCCUPATION of many who make observations about the church is to point out the many things wrong, one almost has to shift mental gears completely to think in terms of what is right with the church. While I confess to be one of the severe critics of many things seen in most churches today, I am also optimistically impressed with much about the church today.

In the first place whatever is said to the contrary, most churches are trying valiantly to remain true to their original objective which is regarded as a divine mandate. This is to bring man to God and meaningful life through Jesus Christ. Denominations, or churches within the same denomination, differ slightly and sometimes more than slightly as to how this objective can most effectively be realized, but they are mostly united in their chief goal. Churches often differ on many doctrinal positions but in the main they are holding to the changeless truths as disclosed by God in Jesus Christ and recorded in the Scriptures.

Another thing right about the church today is its greater and greater concern for persons instead of for programs and statistics. In the past too many churches have sat and waited for people to come to them and too many still do. However, it's clearly discernible today that the church is determined to reach out and find people where they are, accept them for what they are and testify to what they can be when properly related to God through Jesus Christ.

The church today is also right in demonstrating more and more flexibility in the choice of means and methods in accomplishing its task. In spite of some expected reluctance and resistance to change, most concerned churchmen demonstrate more and more openness to fresh, creative and experimental ways to communicate its eternal message to the non-churched and to those who are already church members but are disenchanted with past attitudes and stances of church leadership. In many churches today there is surprisingly growing openness toward making place for zealous youth and lay groups which have been on the verge of writing off the established and institutionalized church.

The church today is right in engaging more and more in an honest and sincere effort to apply the truth it has proclaimed through the centuries to the critical issues that confront contemporary society. It is not true of all active and sincere members but more and more church members today see the vital relationship between religious convictions stemming from the teachings of Jesus and such issues as racial reconciliation, justice in political and economic structures, relief of poverty and its attendant blights and conservation of God-given natural resources and physical environment.

My observations are understandably somewhat limited to Southern Baptists with whom I try to minister in making known to all the reconciling love of God. In spite of our image of being one of the most conservative and reactionary major denominations in America so far as change is concerned, I see many encouraging signs of concern not only for a person-to-person witness but for applying the message of Jesus Christ to all structures that affect mankind whether they be social, economic, political, religious or otherwise.

One illustration from Southern Baptists is offered to support this observation. Not only did Southern Baptists officially adopt several years ago one of the strongest and most forthright statements of concern for racial reconciliation but a growing number of churches have been engaging in redemptive racial reconciliation. As far back as 1968 a survey revealed 3,400 Southern Baptist churches either had already or were willing to accept black members and the number has greatly increased since then. This doesn't sound impressive to those expecting overnight changes, but it represents much progress in light of our past record. Recent surveys reveal that over 80 percent of Southern Baptists would welcome blacks into their worship services and over 70 percent would accept blacks into their fellowship.

Though we have a long way to go to reach the expectations of the Lord of the Church as found in the New Testament and the picture of the early church found in Acts puts us to shame, there is much reason for hope for the church tomorrow. (February 19, 1972)

THE NECESSITY OF TRUE REPENTANCE
IN REGENERATION

FROM A REVERED, RETIRED PREACHER HAS COME
a suggestion that an editorial be written on the subject "The
Place of Repentance in Redemption." His request is based on the
concern that this is largely a missing element in much preaching
today. He laments that many public invitations to accept Christ
either do not include pointing out the necessity of repentance
toward God or do not explain what it means to repent according
to the New Testament.

The importance of repentance in a true relationship with God
is demonstrated, as this concerned former pastor and missionary
points out, in that the word "repent" in some form appears more
than 100 times in the Bible. The danger in not explaining the
meaning of true repentance in God's invitation to redemption is
illustrated by this preacher's experience who says he was a
church member four years before being redeemed.

Ordinary doctrinal dissertation is used on other than editorial
pages of the *Western Recorder*. In this instance, however, there is
enough justification in this brother's concern to merit an exception. It is this writer's observation that most Baptist preachers
understand the meaning of true repentance and it is not an
unheard note in their preaching but it is not emphasized nearly
enough. The result is an easy-sounding invitation that can make
for a shallow experience which withers like the plants from seed
sown on the stony soil in the parable of Jesus. This is one explanation why one of every two persons who join Baptist churches
are not to be found in any meaningful life of the church within
one year and several of the more than 11 million Southern
Baptists we have on church rolls cannot be found anywhere and
many more demonstrate no fruits of regeneration.

There are two Greek words in the New Testament which are
translated "repentance." One means sorrow or regret for some

decision or act but does not necessarily involve a change in the person that means a new way of life. The other word means a change of mind on the part of the person that results in a change of conduct and a permanent new way of life.

Judas and Simon Peter illustrate these two kinds of regret. Judas regretted betraying Jesus and tried to return the 30 pieces of silver but never truly repented and died at his own hands out of fellowship with God. Peter, on the other hand, regretted denying his association with Jesus, repented truly of his sin, and was forgiven and became the preacher at Pentecost and the leader of the early church.

Paul in writing to the Corinthian Christians in 2 Corinthians 7:8-10 uses both these words for repentance and clearly shows the difference. In verse eight, he refers to his chastising of them in his earlier letter and says he did not repent (regret) of chastising them because it led them to repent (change their minds and ways). In verse 10, Paul differentiates between godly sorrow which produces a repentance leading to salvation and a worldly sorrow which leads to death. There are signs that too many who respond to easy invitations to be saved experience worldly sorrow but not godly sorrow.

A person can regret the way he is living until the day he dies and never really repent. On the other hand, if he truly repents he cannot go on living the way he once lived though he will fall many times but will seek and receive forgiveness.

In our invitations we are not careful always to link true repentance with faith. According to the New Testament the two go together and one is impossible apart from the other. Paul made this clear when reviewing his ministry in Ephesus to the elders who met him at Miletus. He reminded them that he had not failed to declare publicly and from house to house anything that was profitable "testifying both to Jews and to Greeks of repentance to God and of faith in our Lord Jesus Christ." (Acts 20:21 RSV)

Repentance and faith then are two facets of the same experience. We cannot turn to Jesus as Savior and Lord without changing our mind and turning from the way we once lived. Furthermore, both ability to repent truly and trust sincerely are the gifts of God's grace.

To explain repentance and to demonstrate regeneration with such an understanding of repentance might not produce as impressive statistics as we now report but will make more impression upon this dubious but hungry generation for religion that makes a difference. (September 18, 1971)

OBSERVATIONS ON SPEAKING IN TONGUES

ONE OF THE MOST PUZZLING PHENOMENA IN religion today is glossolalia (speaking in tongues). Until about 15 years ago tongue-speaking was almost exclusively associated with churches such as Pentecostal, Assemblies of God and Church of God. Today it cuts across all denominational lines and numbers among its followers Roman Catholics, Episcopalians, Presbyterians, Methodists, Baptists and members of every kind of church.

This easy and widespread moving across denominational lines has led some observers to call it the most unifying force among today's denominations. Glossolaliacs often feel closer in fellowship with one another than they feel toward members of their own congregation.

It is ironical, however, that with Southern Baptists it is the most divisive and controversial force of this period. It has resulted in alienation of church members from one another, church splits and even the exclusion of tongue-speaking churches from Baptist district associations in Texas and Ohio. Tongue speaking generally can be handled without tearing up a church unless the pastor is involved. When he is involved as a speaker in tongues, a church split generally results.

Kentucky Baptist churches have not been invaded by tongue-speaking as much as churches in some other states but it is widespread enough that it cannot be ignored. Church members caught in tongue-speaking situations are confused and don't know which way to go. This is understandable since there is no precedent or established policy on treatment of tongue-speaking in Baptist churches. Sincere Baptists don't want to miss anything good but they don't want to go off the deep end.

For this reason this editorial and at least one other are offered to help church members deal with this phenomenon. Readers are cautioned to remember this is only the editor's position and he speaks for no other Baptist.

The following are observations on tongue-speaking as I see it in Paul's words to the church at Corinth where tongue-speaking had become a serious problem.

Tongue-speaking apparently was considered a valid gift by Paul. He expressed no surprise that tongue-speaking was being practiced in the church at Corinth. His concern was not the use but the abuse of tongues.

Tongues were considered a gift from the Holy Spirit. Else why would Paul list it with other gifts of the Spirit?

Tongues were not the gift of the Holy Spirit but a gift among others. There is no reason to believe all Christians are to expect the gift of tongues.

Tongues was the least of all gifts according to Paul. He urged Corinthian believers to seek the gift of prophesying because five words in understandable language are worth more than 10,000 in unintelligible sound.

Tongues in Corinth were different from the foreign languages spoken in Jerusalem on Pentecost day. In Jerusalem hearers heard the gospel in their own language. In Corinth hearers could not understand the ecstatic utterances and were confused instead of helped.

Tongues were not to be prohibited but to be carefully controlled. A maximum of two or three tongue-speakers was allowed for each service and only then if interpreters were present.

Tongues were for the strengthening of the individual believer personally. They were more appropriate in private prayer and personal worship than in public worship services.

Tongues were not necessary for a complete and fully dedicated life. Some believers received the gift of tongues, others didn't. There is no record of the 3,000 converts on Pentecost day having received tongues.

Tongues are no reason for spiritual pride. This was exactly the problem in Corinth. The Corinthian tongue-speakers regarded those without the tongue gift as second-class believers.

Tongues as all other gifts of the Holy Spirit were given to glorify Jesus Christ and to edify the church. Tongues in Corinth were doing neither of these, nor are congregations today who argue and split over tongue-speaking. (May 13, 1976)

PREACHERS' INHUMANITY TO PREACHERS

MAN'S INHUMANITY TO MAN IS NOWHERE more evident than in the ministry. Preachers are probably harder on one another than most any other group.

Every preacher some time or another has the opportunity to pass judgment on his fellow preacher. When he does, he faces two dangers. One is to say good things that are not true or to withhold known facts. The other is to say bad things based on rumor or on superficial knowledge.

Preachers are not perfect. The call of God does not remove our humanity. We make mistakes which should be forgiven when confessed. On the other hand, some preachers have unconfessed sins that follow them and come to the surface wherever they go. They hurt him and usually hurt the church he serves even more. These ought not to be concealed by those asked about him if they are actually known.

For example, if a preacher leaves unpaid debts wherever he goes, this ought to be known by the church about to call him. To withhold known facts which a church ought to know about a preacher is to be dishonest. This doesn't mean that every mistake a man has ever made must be recounted.

A greater wrong than concealing facts to make a preacher look good is unjust criticism that makes him look bad. This is generally called "blackballing" and too much of it goes on. It's about the meanest, lowest and most un-Christian thing one can do.

Nowhere should we be more careful than when talking about a minister of God. His ministry depends upon his reputation. Preachers are especially vulnerable to gossip and just a few words can destroy him.

Preachers really don't have time to know much about each other if they take care of their own flocks. The most they know is what they hear, and this is never reliable. The truth is that when one speaks evil of another, he is often trying to cover a flaw in his own character. Envy or insecurity often motivates criticism of others. A good policy when asked about someone else, preacher or otherwise, is to say all the good we know and remain silent on second-hand information. If we feel constrained to pass on something critical, we should check it out carefully before doing so.

A critical word about another may seem like a harmless thing. Only a few will ever know. But what could be more evil than to destroy one's ministry with careless or irresponsible words? (August 12, 1965)

SEXUAL IMMORALITY IN THE MINISTRY

S EXUAL IMMORALITY IS A GROWING PROBLEM IN the Baptist ministry. It is painful to say such a thing but the problem is prevalent enough that it must be faced and dealt with.

In the last several weeks one pastor and one staff member of Baptist churches in Kentucky have been found guilty of adultery and another pastor has deserted his wife for another woman. In two of these instances the second parties in the affairs were staff members of Baptist institutions. It would serve no redemptive purpose to reveal names and places but it also serves no redemptive purpose to ignore such shameful and destructive conduct and sweep it under the rug. Recognition of the problem should serve as a warning to other ministers when tempted.

There is no way to calculate the damage of such conduct. It virtually destroys the minister involved and his family. It tears a church apart and it tragically hurts the faith of church members and especially young people. It reflects upon every minister, every church and every true believer.

If the angels in heaven rejoice over every soul born into the Kingdom of God, the demons in hell dance with glee over every minister who falls into adultery. Adultery is no more sinful in a preacher than in anyone else but it is far more damaging because of his exalted and influential position.

How is such conduct on the part of God's special servants explained? One explanation is that ministers are human and are subject to the same temptations as anyone else. In fact, the sexual temptation is intensified for ministers who in counseling and other relationships deal one-to-one with women, some of whom seem to delight in seeing how far the minister will go.

No doubt the permissive spirit of modern society and the exploitation of sex in every area of American life affect a minister as it does everyone else.

But neither these nor any other reason justify a moral lapse by a minister. Not even the rationalization that some ministers have unhappy marriages excuses such conduct.

How should a church deal with a pastor or staff member involved in adultery? If the guilty minister denies what he has done or tries to conceal it, he must be exposed and removed forthrightly. If he confesses and asks for forgiveness, he should be forgiven but not lightly. The forgiveness should include redemptive help in salvaging his ministry, if he feels he should, but not in the church where the offense occurred.

It is inconceivable a minister could ever recover enough credibility and influence to continue ministering in the church or community where he committed adultery. The most he could expect would be forgiveness and an opportunity to salvage his ministry somewhere else. Moreover, he would have to be honest with any other church considering him.

What can be done to help prevent a minister from falling into adultery? Whatever anyone else can do to help, the primary responsibility is upon the minister himself. He cannot always control situations which bring temptations but he can decide firmly beforehand what he will do when tempted. If he does not have enough self-control to resist the temptation of adultery, he should get out or should never have gotten into the ministry.

A minister should never underestimate the power of Satan but always remember the Apostle Peter's characterization of the devil as "a roaring lion, (who) walketh about, seeking whom he may devour." A minister is a prime target of Satan so he should begin every day with a sincere prayer for the help of the Holy Spirit in every situation he will encounter and at the end of every day thank the Lord for bringing him safely through the day.

In ordination examinations and services a minister should be helped to see the imperative of a pure heart as well as pure doctrine. He should be required to commit himself to orthodox behavior as well as orthodox theology.

Colleges and seminaries where ministers are trained should bear down on moral rectitude as unqualified prerequisite for ministers of God.

Above all, church members should pray for their ministers every day. (September 27, 1978)

A NEW DIMENSION OF CHRISTIAN EXPERIENCE

IF A FEW YEARS AGO SOMEONE HAD PREDICTED A Roman Catholic archbishop and a Baptist pastor would be roommates at Cedarmore and that Catholic priests and Baptist preachers in a joint worship service would be singing "On Jordan's Stormy Banks I Stand" he would have been considered ready to be institutionalized. I saw exactly that last week and there was nothing artificial or strained about it.

The occasion was the first Baptist-Roman Catholic dialogue on the state level in Kentucky history. It was one of those experiences which was deeply satisfying for the participants but which cannot be adequately described to those who were not involved.

The fact is many *Western Recorder* readers will not be convinced that anything good can come from dialogue between Baptists and Catholics. This was my own feeling much of my life. This feeling is understandable in light of our historic understanding of the Catholic view of salvation and their attitude toward non-Catholics.

But Catholicism has undergone profound changes since John XXIII and the Second Vatican Council. Before this council what happened at Cedarmore last week would have been impossible. The decree on ecumenism coming out of this council changed Catholicism almost overnight. This change was as perplexing to many Roman Catholics as it was to non-Catholics. Enough time has elapsed by now to prove the change is real and anyone considering it a ploy or strategy to entice and swallow up non-Catholics is hard put for any proof.

The initiative for this project came from the Catholics and God forbid that we should ever pass up any sincere invitation to talk about our Christian convictions. Baptists have never been reluctant to give reasons for their faith. If our beliefs and convictions are not strong enough to survive and benefit from dialogue with other religious groups, we are not what we claim.

The dialogue experience proved Catholics are willing to come a long way to relate to Baptists. The joint worship services could have passed for worship services in most any Baptist church. We sang from the *Baptist Hymnal*, read scriptures from the King James and modern translations and, from the form and content of spontaneous prayers, one could not tell whether a priest or a Baptist pastor was praying. The Catholics participated enthusiastically in the worship services though they had no elements of the mass which is central in Catholic worship.

There was an amazing openness and warmness from the very beginning of the dialogue. There was an unmistakable spiritual dimension which left participants feeling this is the way it ought to be with fellow Christians by whatever label they are known.

Don't get the wrong impression. Dialogue was frank and honest. There was no compromise of basic convictions of either group. This was never the purpose of the experience.

Baptists and Roman Catholics had fundamental doctrinal differences which cannot be ignored nor minimized by any amount of dialogue. But these differences can be much better understood and in the process some misconceptions can be corrected. We discovered Catholics have about as many misconceptions about Baptists as we have about them.

Perhaps the most profitable results of the dialogue were genuine Christian fellowship and better knowledge of each other's true beliefs and practices. It was inspiring to hear Catholic priests testify to their personal experiences of grace, to learn Catholics do not worship Mary though she is highly venerated by many and, as a Baptist, to feel accepted as a true brother in Christ instead of an alien of the Roman Church outside of which is no salvation.

Those with an openness to new knowledge and new dimensions of Christian fellowship would benefit from properly structured Baptist-Catholic dialog on the local level. (October 3, 1979)

DALEY OBSERVATIONS ON FAMILY

WESTERN RECORDER

YOU CAN GO HOME AGAIN

IN THE HUMAN HEART THERE IS AN ETERNAL longing to go home again. The trouble is that when we try, we generally learn we can't go home again. When we get back where home was it's not the way we left it. Nothing seems quite the same because we are not the same and childhood scenes have long since changed. The old house has fallen in, parents have moved away or passed away and many other happy voices are now silent, having moved to the city of the dead. Even the fields and streams are not near so romantic nor the flowers so fragrant.

But thank the Lord there are exceptions to the rule that you can't go home again. For the goodness of God some of us still can come wonderfully near really going home. Such was my happy experience in recent days.

For me going home means covering the long distance from Louisville to a little farm home in a rural section of South

Georgia. It's the same little farm home nestled in the same pecan grove where my happy, carefree childhood days were spent. Some changes have come like the electric lights and plumbing, but much remains the same. The open fireplace still provides its inexpressible experience with the crackling of the dry wood and the quiet simmering sound of the green oak with its syrupy sap oozing out of the logs' ends. In the front room is the same old high wooden bedstead that must have been an antique when I first remember it 40 or more years ago. Beneath its quilts on a cold night in an unheated room is heavenly rest.

Not far from the house stands the log barn in whose loft on many a rainy day we romped on the hay. Nearer to the house is the bird dog pen, always an important part of the scene. From the back porch the flat fields stretch out to the distant pine trees in the woodland.

What really makes this home for me, however, is not all these but my Mother and Daddy who by the grace of God are still on the farm and able to carry on in spite of the toll of more than 70 years of life and the toil and rigors of tilling the soil.

What on earth can be so exhilarating? To hit the cold floor before dawn after a night of dreaming of fields and woods, dogs and flying quail and a Daddy of 70 still able to out-walk and out-shoot his son. To put on socks and pull on boots in front of the glowing fire is a luxury beyond price. And then to the table still close to the fireplace for breakfast of old ham, grits, gravy, baked sweet potatoes, corn hoe cakes and homemade pear preserves.

After breakfast the dogs, bounding with desire and energy, can't wait to get their chance to show their stuff. But wait they must because before we reached the place we planned to hunt first, a covey of quail was crossing the dirt road into the adjoining corn-field. It was just like I had dreamed. As they flushed from the field to return to their thicket home, three fell with three shots from my 20 gauge. My luck held out on the next covey as I got three more without missing, but from then on the average dropped sharply.

Long before noon the sun had warmed the November day
and this city dweller was tired. After a bountiful dinner and a
short nap it was off again. The quail were still plentiful but wild.
With the setting sun came the evening chill and home and fireplace made a welcome sight again. After supper came the long
remembered quail counting and cleaning in front of the hearth.
Beside the same fireplace where for 50 years thousands of these
beautiful and delectable birds along with wild turkeys and ducks
have been prepared, we counted the exact daily limit of 24 for the
two of us and prepared them for some happy occasion later.

Who said you can't go home again? By the grace of God I
went home again and it was wonderful. As long as I can go home,
I will be grateful. When I can't I'll be grateful for the memories.
(December 9, 1965)

THE LORD IS GOOD

OCCASIONALLY A MAN WRITES FROM HIS HEART
as well as from his head. This is one of those occasions
because it is a special week in the life of the editor and his family.
My father and mother observed their golden wedding anniversary on December 6. By the Lord's goodness they still live on the
little farm in south Georgia where my happy boyhood days were
spent.

There is really no way to value a Christian home and godly
parents. I cannot conceive of life as I know it apart from what my
parents gave me. My earliest memories have to do with Sunday
School on Sunday afternoons, preaching services the second
Sunday each month and preachers hunting and fishing with my
Daddy and staying in our three-room farm home.

I narrowly missed the experience of never knowing my father.
I was born in 1918, the year of the great flu epidemic. My Daddy
was one of its victims and came to the very edge of death with

double-pneumonia in the days of no miracle drugs. Only by the skill of dedicated doctors and the healing miracle of the Lord did he come through. A deep, ugly scar in his back remains where the doctors operated in order to release an unbelievable amount of fluid from both lungs. Part of the little farm had to be sold to pay the bills for the long hospital experience.

Educational opportunities in the early days of my parents were extremely limited, but my Daddy made good use of what little he received. He taught a Sunday School class, served as Sunday School superintendent and as a deacon in our home church.

Two things have marked his life, honesty and hard work. A little fellow in size, he is as strong and tough as the scrub oaks he still cuts for the fireplace. His hours always have been from sun-up to sundown, and he has turned every inch of soil on the farm a thousand or more times. Now past 72, he raised his own crop this year along with cows and hogs and plans to do the same next year.

If he knows more about anything than he does about farming, it's hunting and fishing. It's a saying around home that he can catch fish out of a tub of clear water where there are no fish. Deer, wild turkey, quail and ducks were more common at home when I was a child than store-bought bacon and hot dogs.

His ethics as a sportsman have become a treasured part of my life. For example, he taught me never to touch a fishing line that was left set by someone else. Many times I have seen him go past a set line with a big catfish pulling on it but would not touch it. He also is the only man I ever hunted with who believes only one hunter should shoot each single bird. He says if a quail gets away from one man, the bird deserves to live. This may be because for many years of his hunting experience he was a crack shot and not one in 20 ever got away. He can still get three on a covey rise, as he did the last time we hunted. And in walking the fields and woods, he can outlast his city-soft son.

My mother has always had one handicap: she is blind, that is to any faults of her only son. She saw to it that he was in Sunbeams and then in the Royal Ambassadors when the WMU still had the boys. She was WMU president for more than a quarter of a century and taught a class of young people in Sunday School for many years.

Hard work has been her life also. Long hours over a cook stove, a scrub board, canning, raising chickens and turkeys and often side by side with Daddy in the fields have taken their toll. She won't stop even now with poor health and diminished strength.

Mother and Daddy prayed to be left to live together 50 years. Their prayers are answered. I have often prayed that because they lived sacrificially in order to give their son an opportunity, I might someday help them. So far my prayer is unanswered in that it is they who are still doing the helping, and I am receiving.

They gave whatever they had for the education of their son. They also helped in the education of their first grandson, who this year got his M.D. degree. They have been as generous in other directions, and consequently they have little of this world's possessions. Their bank account is small, their wardrobe is limited and their home is modest, though comfortable. Theirs is the true wealth of living to help others.

As the Psalmist said, "The Lord is good." He seems to be better to some than to others, and I am among those to whom he has been most generous. (December 7, 1967)

THE BENEDICTIONS OF DEATH

THE VALLEY OF THE SHADOW OF DEATH HAS ITS
own blessings. One of the comforting blessings in the recent
death of my mother was the confirmation of truths not always
observable when life is all sunshine.

God's mercy was never more evident than in the way he took
my mother from this world of suffering to that life that knows no
pain. Afflicted with a fatal illness that brought more and more
suffering, we dreaded a prolonged period of intense suffering and
slow death.

But in God's mercy it was not an agonizing struggle for her to
die. Mother ate an evening meal, talked rationally with family
members and went to sleep. Sometime before the next morning
she lapsed into a coma and knew no suffering the remaining three
days she breathed.

God's provision for broken hearts was never so real. Being
blessed with a closely knit family and with parents living to a ripe
old age, I have known no suffering of separation from intimates
until now. But as God has been our strength in life, so is he in death.

In the last hours Daddy kissed Mother and said, "We have
been sweethearts for 65 years." He talked of their school days
when they were almost expelled for writing love notes to one
another and recalled their one little falling out during courtship
which made reunion sweeter. Neither ever had any other serious
sweetheart. What more could a husband ask for?

Sorrow for me was great because love was deep. But who
could ask for more for his mother? Hers was a full and happy life.
Much of it was in difficult times which sometimes found her side-
by-side Daddy in the fields in order to provide necessities of life
and to save the little farm. But much of it was in happy and carefree days along the banks and streams fishing and picnicking with
family and friends.

The God of our lives together was also our providing God in our earlier separation.

Mother's death also revealed the close ties of other members of her and Daddy's families. They came from long distances and busy schedules to express their love and sorrow. I was overwhelmed with gratitude and with some feeling of guilt. I have not always been so thoughtful toward my relatives.

My own sons met some of their relatives for the first time. It was really our first family reunion and we determined not to wait until the death of a loved one to see one another again.

Mother's death was also the occasion to experience the love of the family of God in a way never even imagined. My home church and community in Georgia demonstrated that people still care about one another and express their love in a truly redemptive ministry. Flowers, memorial gifts, food and every other conceivable means of expressing love made the occasion a humbling experience.

In Kentucky and elsewhere the expression of the family of God has been a benediction of healing. By mail, telephone and every other means of communication expressions of love and consolation have been overwhelming. I regret that all of these cannot be individually acknowledged but I hope these sincere words of appreciation will be seen by all who were so gracious.

Finally, I pray my mother's death will make a better man of me. Her many faithful years in her church should call forth more faithful service from her son. Her devotion to the WMU and world missions which resulted in my first little speeches as a Sunbeam and Royal Ambassador should intensify my commitment to world missions. Her warmth and generosity to others should soften my heart and her long-suffering in obstacles should prepare me for any eventuality. I pray that a fraction of the good things said about her can be faithfully said of me at the end of this existence. (March 18, 1976)

DEAR DADDY

YOU AND I HAVE NEVER BEEN MUCH FOR expressing our feelings for each other in words. We have used other means of communication because words never quite capture the deepest sentiments. However, your 79th birthday prompts me to try to put some feelings into words before the one or the other of us says goodbye to this world.

Above all else I thank you for a pattern of life which a son could follow without any reluctance. The honesty, integrity and humility exemplified in your life have inspired me more than any sermon I ever heard. A good example is about the greatest heritage a child can be given and I have never fallen short when I patterned my life after yours.

You never read a book on how to rear children but I can never thank you enough for how you related to me. You trusted me and we were more like buddies than a father and son. You permitted me to make my own decisions from an early age though many of them were wrong. I never feared you as some children fear their fathers. My love for you and my respect for your wisdom are such that I've never made an important decision without seeking your counsel. I regret I have not always been this kind of a father to my sons.

Some of the most vivid memories and lasting influences in my life are from early childhood when we spent endless hours together. It was then I learned the dignity of toil and the sanctity of the soil. I saw what could be wrought by God and a willing man. You always strove for excellence and in spite of too much or too little rain our crops were among the best every year. You taught me never to be content with less than the best no matter how much sweat was required.

I know the blessing of restful sleep after a long, hot day in the fields and the peace of a clean conscience for never cheating. I recall the heartbreak of total loss of a cotton crop from merciless hail and the anxiety of trying to get the crop in before the destructiveness of an approaching tropical hurricane.

My life is infinitely richer and happier for the many hours we spent in the fields and on the streams in quest of game and fish. I remember the afternoon I killed my first wild turkey as if it were yesterday and the inexpressible thrill of a dog on point and a quail on the wing. You are the only hunter I ever knew who always gave the other man the first and best shot but still usually came out with the most birds.

Among my treasures are the sense of fair play toward wildlife and respect for all the wonders of God's creation I learned from you long before I can remember. You taught me never to take a fish from another fisherman's trot line or limb line no matter how tempting it was. You inspired my self-confidence as a marksman as well as demonstrated rare sportsman's ethics when you refused to shoot a bird after I missed it. You always said, "If he gets away from one man, he deserves to live." And many times he did live.

Thank you for determining to give me the opportunity for education and training you never had. You and mother worked side-by-side in the fields in an effort to give me an education so that I would not have to sweat so much to live. Ironically, it seems now to me to have been the good life of much of what you saved me from is what I now long for.

No son ever saw in his father a better example of genuine religion. Faith in God, trust in Jesus Christ and devotion to the church are a way of life with you. Without much formal education you served well as a deacon and superintendent of the Sunday School. Your public prayers were not flowery but sincere. My own Christian faith and concern for God's will in my life were almost an unconscious part of my endowment. I tremble to think where I would be today apart from the spiritual influence of you and mother.

One of the few pains of my life has come from living most of my life so far away from you. Not being around to help when needed and to enjoy just being together has made me examine my call to the ministry many times. You have made it more bearable by not questioning my understanding of God's will and by saying many times in recent years, "If we are never together again in this life, never shoot another quail or catch another fish, the Lord has given us far more than we could ask for or deserve."

As you assess your successes and failures for 79 years, remember you have been to me all an earthly father could be. (October 31, 1979)

FATHER TO OLDEST SON

SO YOU'RE OFF TO COLLEGE, SON. WHILE YOU'RE packing up the rest of your things, tuck away in some corner of your luggage this little bit of advice from your Daddy. It might not seem important now but it could come in handy if you don't wait too long to unpack it.

College attendance is a special privilege and should never be considered otherwise. Thousands in our country and millions over the world will never have the privilege you have today. And you have it only at a high cost to your parents and to many others.

And so this is likely the most important day in your life. The rest of your life depends largely upon how your college experience comes out. Few who fail in college succeed elsewhere, and few who succeed in college fail elsewhere.

The most important thing to remember as you leave home is that you are on your own. You've wanted to be your own boss a long time; now you are. Your parents will not be close enough to say yes or no, and this makes your yes and no far more important. When trying to decide which to say, it might help to remember what your parents would likely say if they were asked.

Even your teachers will leave you mostly on your own. In high school they prodded you about studying; in college they offer it to you and you can take it or leave it. But because they don't push you, don't think they won't hold it against you if you loaf. And remember, what you leave today is almost impossible to pick up tomorrow, all the midnight oil and no-sleep pills notwithstanding.

Soon after you get to school you'll begin to hear that grades are not everything. And that's right, but they're something and you won't be around long if you don't believe it. Don't forget that grades are like Pilate's superscription—they're once-for-all and will help or haunt you as long as you live.

More important than grades are the subjects you select and the teachers you choose. You won't have a choice every time, but when you do, pick the right teachers, for long after the subject matter is forgotten, the influence of your teachers will remain with you. Your college is only as great as the teachers. While on the subject of courses, take them as they come, the hard with the easy. It will only add to your misery to leave the dreaded ones to last.

Don't worry if you still don't know what you want to be or what to major in as you begin your college experience. Take your time and try to be sure when you decide. And when you're deciding, the first consideration ought not be what will bring you the highest salary but what will come near helping this old world overcome some of its ills. How to live is far more important than how to make a living.

But one thing you can surely expect. Your religious views learned in Sunday School will be challenged in college science courses and even in religion courses. This is as it should be for your religious understanding grows also. Wait it out and you'll find true science and true religion support rather than contradict one another.

Don't think it's smart to be an agnostic. There's always two or three in every student body smarting off, sometimes even a faculty member, but it's usually more to attract attention than anything else. Don't give up your own views until you find something better to replace them, and then don't be reluctant.

Have fun but don't confuse fun with folly. You'll find every kind of person to associate with from the best to the worst and you'll meet every temptation in the book before you're there long. Remember the irrevocable law of sowing and reaping, and that in one foolish escapade you can lose all you have saved your whole life. What will it profit you if you gain the whole world of intellect and lose your personal moral purity? Experience is the best teacher, it is true, but some things are better learned from the experiences of others.

What I said to start with, success or failure is largely up to you, but whether you fail or succeed probably matters now more to your Mother and Daddy than to you. We don't believe you will disappoint us. (August 30, 1962)

FATHER TO YOUNGEST SON

AS YOU KNOW, YOUR DAD TRIES TO HIDE HIS emotions. This was the case day before yesterday when your mother and I said goodbye to you in the dormitory parking lot at the college where you are now a first-year student. It was mother who shed the visible tears but tears also filled my heart though I kept them back from my eyes.

I am a little surprised at this and I don't know exactly how to explain it. I don't love you more than I do your three older brothers who one by one have left home for college. Somehow it's different with you. Maybe it's because you are the last child and the house is empty of sights and sounds of children for the first time in 30 years. Maybe one grows more sentimental with age and this is part of the explanation. Whatever the cause for this feeling, I know now what I never really knew before when friends talked about his stage of their life. I also for the first time know what my parents experienced when they said goodbye to me upon leaving for college never to return again except for summer vacations and visits.

The house is so quiet and lonely since you left. A few days ago it wasn't big enough for the loud music of your hi-fi but now it seems far too big. I haven't seen a soft drink bottle or glass of ice on the floor in front of the television since you went away. To be honest I'd like to see your big shoes and socks in the middle of the floor though I have not forgotten fussing about them. The new peas in the garden are ready but they seem hardly worth picking and shelling just for Mother and me. They can't quite say so with words but Toy, the collie, and Charlie, the beagle, keep asking by their actions where you are. They miss the romp with you in the yard every day.

Don't get me wrong. I don't wish you were here. Mother and I are happy and grateful to God that you have chosen further preparation in college. This appreciation is enhanced when we remember you chose to go to college not in hopes of making more money later in life but because you want a greater capacity to appreciate all that life affords and because you feel college training can equip you better for whatever the Lord has in mind for you to do in life.

Another comfort is that we are confident you know how to use the freedom you will have to a degree you never had before. Before you left we didn't give you a long list of do's and dont's because we learned when we went out on our own we had to make our own list and live by our convictions and not those of our parents. As you approached your 18th birthday which we celebrated the day you departed for school you were given more and more freedom to order your own life. All we could ask is that you use it as wisely at college as you did at home.

We have often discussed with you and with your brothers in your presence what college is all about. However, it will not be what you expect. It's a new and wonderful world however it may seem at first. Your teacher will be for you though you could never tell it by the way some of them will appear at first. Their bark is often worse than their bite and they have a purpose behind their ways. Most of your teachers will share our ideals for you though you need to be prepared for an occasional immature or smart-alec teacher who would try to destroy your Christian faith or scoff at your moral ideals.

While we are still thinking about why you are in school, don't forget that you have to be concerned about grades. Grades are an inadequate way to judge progress in education but no better way has been found so far. Don't regard grades so important that you miss all the other values to be found in college. However, it would be tragic to major on extracurricular and fail your academic courses. A large percentage of your class will receive notices half way through the semester that they are failing one or more courses. If you remember that now you are not likely to be one of these.

Here I go giving you advice which you have heard over and over. The end of the whole matter is you are on your own—to succeed or fail. We have confidence in you. After all, you are paying part of your way with money you earned literally by the sweat of your brow. You are borrowing another part of it and will have to pay it back after you finish. Your parents among other things are driving a three-year-old car instead of a new one to help you. On top of this Kentucky Baptists and other supporters of the college are contributing substantially to your college education. However, don't worry too much about meeting the expectations of your parents or other friends. Be more concerned to follow the gleam put in you by our Heavenly Father. (September 16, 1972)

DALEY OBSERVATIONS ON LEADERS

WESTERN RECORDER

EISENHOWER: AN EXAMPLE OF TRUE GREATNESS

THE NATION APPROPRIATELY PAUSED LAST WEEK in grateful tribute to Dwight David Eisenhower. By now nothing has been left unsaid about this magnificent and magnanimous man, but we merely want to say that the tributes of America and the world were never more appropriately directed.

He died as he lived—calmly, confidently and victoriously. His going could have been at no more fitting time than the very time when the world recalls the death and resurrection of Jesus Christ and their hope for humanity.

Ike was the personification of what we regard as an ideal American. He embraced the virtues and ideals associated with true greatness. There can be little sadness in saying farewell to someone who lived so humbly and helpfully and deserved his rest and reward. Any grief which comes is in the realization that America seems to be producing fewer and fewer such men.

Though he served in the most important and powerful places in the nation and the world, he escaped the unfavorable images often associated with those in such high places. He commanded the most powerful war machine and led in the mightiest military victory in history, but he was always a man truly devoted to peace. He was a military man par excellence but never a militarist.

He filled the highest political office in the nation, but was never a politician in the ordinary sense. Unlike too many office-seekers, including even presidential candidates, one never felt he made promises he knew he couldn't keep just to get votes. Neither did he sell himself by trying to tear someone else down.

On the other hand, one felt Ike would do more than he promised instead of less. The kind of confidence and trust he inspired made the existence of a credibility gap unthinkable.

He proved that gentleness is the greatest strength of all, that the path to greatness is the walk of humility and that the truly great man is one whom honor seeks instead of one who seeks honor. Those of us in this generation especially should take note of the useful life and happy end of one who headed his list of values with God, home, family and country.

The best summary of his life is found in his own words. "I have always loved my wife. I have always loved my children. I have always loved my grandchildren. I have always loved my country." About the only thing he could have added would have been, "I have always loved my God." This was unnecessary, however, because he said this more eloquently in his life than he ever could have in words. (April 10, 1969)

THE RELIGION OF ABRAHAM LINCOLN

ABRAHAM LINCOLN, WHOSE BIRTHDAY WE celebrate in February, is my all-time favorite president. His humble birth in a long cabin in the frontier land of Kentucky, his lifelong link with the common people, his meteoric rise to fame, his agonizing years as president, his courageous Emancipation Proclamation and his untimely assassination all made him an inspiring hero for me from boyhood days on.

In spite of my lifelong admiration for Lincoln and the abundance of written material on all aspects of his life, I have not done enough reading and research to know him very well. Somewhere along the line, however, I got a disappointing impression he had little place for formal religion and the church.

Because of my disappointment at this point I was elated to read recently an article in *Pulpit Helps* written by Lincoln scholar Ronald D. Rietvelt, professor of history at California State University. Prof. Rietvelt dealt with the spiritual side of Lincoln. From his own words and from impressions of those closest to Lincoln as reported by the professor, it is clear Lincoln was not only a man who recognized God but he leaned strongly upon the Lord for divine guidance and help.

Upon leaving Springfield, Ill., February 11, 1861, for Washington, Lincoln had some farewell words for his friends and neighbors. He ended his brief speech with these words, "Here my children were born, and one is buried. I leave now, not knowing when, or whether ever I may return, with a task before me greater than that which rested upon Washington. Without the assistance of that Divine Being who ever attended him, I cannot fail. Trusting in him who can go with me, and remain with you and be everywhere for good, let us confidently hope that all will be well. To his care commending you, as I hope in your prayers you will commend me, I bid you an affectionate farewell."

Upon saying goodbye to his pastor friend a few days earlier, Lincoln had made this request: "I wish to be remembered in the prayers of yourself and our church members."

Lincoln prayed that the war might be averted but when it came he took the view that God "permits it for some wise purpose of his own, mysterious and unknown to us; and though with our limited understanding we may not be able to comprehend it, yet we cannot but believe that he who made the world still governs it."

In 1862 while the war was still going against the North, Lincoln suffered probably the greatest personal sorrow of his life. His little son, Willie, died. The president had watched beside Willie's bed throughout the night, and after the boy died Lincoln pulled the cover from the child's face and whispered, "My poor boy; He was too good for this earth. God has called him home, I know that he is much better off in heaven, but then we loved him so. It is hard, hard to have him die."

When Willie's Christian nurse tried to reassure Lincoln that many Christians were praying for him, he replied with tear-filled eyes: "I am glad to hear that. I want them to pray for me. I need to have that. I want them to pray for me. I need their prayers."

The president said to the nurse, "I will try to go to God with my sorrows. ... I wish I had that childlike faith you speak of, and I trust he will give it to me. I had a good Christian mother, and her prayers have followed me thus far through life."

Being worried about the effect of the death of Willie upon the mental and physical health of her husband, Mrs. Lincoln invited Francis Vinton, minister of Trinity Church, New York, to visit Lincoln. In trying to console the president Dr. Vinton said: "Your son is alive in paradise. Do you remember that passage in the Gospels, 'God is not the God of the dead but the living, for all line unto him'?"

The president embraced Dr. Vinton, laid his head upon his shoulders and sobbed, "Alive! Alive!"

As the war continued to go against the Union forces and casualty lists grew longer, President Lincoln confided in a friend, "I have been driven many times upon my knees by the overwhelming conviction I had nowhere else to go."

Praying seemed to become a way of life with President Lincoln. One of his secretaries reported: "Mr. Lincoln was a praying man. I know that to be a fact, and I have heard him request people to pray for him, ... I have heard him say he prayed."

His pastor in Washington, Dr. Phineas Gurley, said of Lincoln, "In the latter days of his chastened and weary life, after the death of his son Willie and his visit to Gettysburg, he said, with tears in his eyes, that he had lost confidence in everything but God and that he now believed his heart was changed and that he loved the Savior."

Lincoln told one of his friends, Noah Brooks, that he had hope of blessed immortality through Jesus Christ and that the change in his life had occurred after coming to Washington.

The longer he lived the more Lincoln was convinced he was a God-chosen instrument for such a day as his own. Shortly before his assassination he affirmed, "I am responsible ... to the American people, to the Christian world and, on my final account, to God."

President Lincoln's formal religion and church life might not have met our ideals but his words above leave no doubt he was a spiritual man and looked to God for wisdom and help.

Lincoln's honest struggles with a personal faith sound more authentic than glib claims of religious convictions mouthed by presidents but written by their speech writers. (February 9, 1983)

A PROPHET IN HIS OWN COUNTRY

KENTUCKIANS ARE PROUD ABRAHAM LINCOLN came from the Knob country of Kentucky. Our hearts beat a little faster, our eyes become misty and our spines tingle every time we see the crude log cabin which sheltered him and his family from the snow and cold of Kentucky winters.

We like to think that Lincoln's concern for the common man, his compassion for the enslaved and his commitment to preserve the union were all a part of his Kentucky roots.

Lincoln's greatness of mind and spirit might have been rooted in frontier Kentucky but, if so, most of his contemporaries in his native land did not share his feelings or convictions. Turning through a history of Hardin County recently, I came across a reference to Lincoln and his election as President in 1860. Larue County, the site of the Lincoln cabin now, was a part of Hardin County in 1860. The history says Lincoln received only four votes for the presidency in Hardin County in 1860.

Jesus said nothing more profoundly true than this: "No prophet is accepted in his own country" (Luke 4:24). He found this true in his hometown of Nazareth and so have most of those who have been prophets.

Being prophetic and being popular usually don't go together. The religious establishment of every age has a way of rejecting prophets. It equates tradition with truth and regards it as the final and absolute revelation. A prophet is usually a dissenter and is rejected. He is often persecuted as a heretic. So it was not only with Jesus but with John the Baptist, John Calvin, Martin Luther, John Knox and other heroes of the Christian faith.

History reveals that the majority has often been wrong though it claimed the leadership of the Holy Spirit. The voice of the people has not always proved to be the voice of God.

One who is especially sensitive to the spiritual and moral teachings of Jesus often has to stand alone or with the minority. There is something sad about this.

Surely not all dissenters are heroes and not all who disagree with the majority are right. But the lesson of history should reassure those who have to take the unpopular stand on grounds of conscience. It should also teach us to be more open and more tolerant of those who disagree with us.

Lincoln received only four votes in his home county but no greater has ever sat in the president's chair. One generation rejects the prophet whom the next generation rises up to call blessed. (October 4, 1975)

MY LINES HAVE FALLEN IN PLEASANT PLACES

IN REFLECTING UPON 27 YEARS AS *WESTERN Recorder* editor, my testimony is that of the psalmist, "The lines are fallen unto me in pleasant places." I leave the editorial responsibilities for other ministries with a mind full of happy remembrances and a heart full of thanksgiving.

My gratitude is first of all to Kentucky Baptists, a great people of God by every standard. They have been gracious, kind and above all tolerant of one whose editorial positions have frequently been contrary to majority opinion. This is a mark of greatness.

One of the greatest rewards of denominational service is to come to know the choicest of God's children in hundreds of Baptist congregations. My wealth in this respect is incalculable and because of knowing these faithful ones I could never be pessimistic about the future of God's cause in Kentucky.

My editorial ministry could never have been without the help of *Western Recorder* directors provided by the convention. Over the years many outstanding Baptist ministers and laypersons have served as directors and have supported me completely. They have granted me total freedom, which is a dangerous but absolutely essential possession for an effective editor.

I am equally indebted to excellent staff members who have taken much of the load off my shoulders. My associate editors have in every instance been outstanding and at least two of them have gone on to be outstanding editors of other state papers.

My present associate, Jim Cox, is the answer to an editor's dream. He does about everything but write the editorials and, fortunately for the editor, has no ambition to be an editorial writer. He is a master technician and an effective teacher of journalism skills.

All other workers in the *Western Recorder* offices have been as helpful as coworkers could be. I shall never be able to pay my debt to Juanita Spicer, who has served as my secretary for many years and by now is a miracle performer in reading my writing and processing my correspondence and my editorials. George Strickland has set our type and put our paper together for many years. By now he knows my mind as well as I do and his judgments on headlines and other details are better than mine.

My colleagues in the Baptist Building have been extremely supportive. Many times they have not gotten as much space in the paper as they wanted and deserved but they have always been understanding and forgiving. The four executive secretary-treasurers with whom I have served have been dear friends and helpful counselors. In 27 years there have not been many disagreements and not a single serious rift between the executive secretary and the editor.

My greatest human debt is to Christine, my mate who many times served as father and mother for our four sons while I placed *Western Recorder* interests before family responsibilities. She has suffered from my frustrations for which she was not responsible and has been the object of hostilities which I concealed from those arousing them. She has also been my most faithful supporter and most valuable critic.

It's understandable that I leave such a happy and fulfilling ministry from my standpoint with mixed feelings. I have never doubted, however, the rightness of leaving it now and turning to other kingdom services. Whatever these are and wherever they lead, I shall be eternally grateful to Kentucky Baptists for making my lines fall in pleasant places. (June 26, 1984)

INDEX

(Provides initial page numbers only for multi-paged entries)

173